THE ART OF

SPIRITUAL

HEALING

WRITINGS OF JOEL S. GOLDSMITH

The Art of Meditation
Practicing the Presence
The Infinite Way
Living the Infinite Way
Spiritual Interpretation of Scripture
The Letters
Conscious Union with God
Consciousness Unfolding
God the Substance of All Form
Infinite Way Letters 1955
Infinite Way Letters 1956
Infinite Way Letters 1957
Infinite Way Letters 1958
Infinite Way Letters 1959
The Art of Spiritual Healing

THE ART OF
SPIRITUAL
HEALING

BY JOEL S. GOLDSMITH

HARPER & ROW, PUBLISHERS

NEW YORK, HAGERSTOWN,
SAN FRANCISCO, LONDON

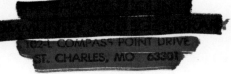

Except the Lord build the house, they
labour in vain that build it.
—Psalm 127

Illumination dissolves all material ties and binds men
together with the golden chains of spiritual understanding; it acknowledges only the leadership of the Christ;
it has no ritual or rule but the divine, impersonal universal Love; no other worship than the inner Flame
that is ever lit at the shrine of Spirit. This union is the
free state of spiritual brotherhood. The only restraint
is the discipline of Soul, therefore we know liberty
without license; we are a united universe without
physical limits; a divine service to God without ceremony or creed. The illumined walk without fear—
by Grace.

—THE INFINITE WAY

CONTENTS

PART ONE

SPIRITUAL HEALING: THE PRINCIPLES

I	*What Is Spiritual Healing?*	11
II	*Is God a Servant?*	21
III	*One Power*	32
IV	*The Language of Spiritual Healing*	40
V	*What Did Hinder You?*	56

PART TWO

SPIRITUAL HEALING: THE ROLE OF TREATMENT

VI	*Developing a Healing Consciousness*	73
VII	*Practical Instructions to Workers*	82
VIII	*Treatment Is a Realization of Omnipresence*	93

PART THREE

SPIRITUAL HEALING: THE PRACTICE

IX	*What About This Body?*	105
X	*Spiritual Unfoldment—Not Human Birth or Death*	113
XI	*The Relationship of Oneness*	124
XII	*God Is Our Destiny*	135
XIII	*A New Concept of Supply*	142
XIV	*Under the Shadow of the Almighty*	154

PART FOUR

SPIRITUAL HEALING: WITHOUT WORDS OR THOUGHTS

XV	*Beyond Words and Thoughts*	167
XVI	*Is*	175
XVII	*If I Be Lifted Up*	183

PART ONE

SPIRITUAL
HEALING:

THE PRINCIPLES

CHAPTER I

WHAT IS SPIRITUAL HEALING?

The world is not in need of a new religion, nor is the world in need of a new philosophy: What the world needs is healing and regeneration. The world needs people who, through devotion to God, are so filled with the Spirit that they can be the instruments through which healings take place, because healing is important to everybody.

Until the last century, healing had been considered largely the prerogative of the medical profession; but in recent years, so many churches have turned their attention to this subject that today the healing of mind, body, and personal relationships is beginning to be considered as much the function of the church as of the doctor's office. Churches are opening their doors to discussions of the possibility of healing through prayer and other means. Other organizations are being formed for the purpose of engaging in research and in promoting the study and practice of various forms of healing, ranging all the way from spiritual healing to psychological and psychic healing. More and more, spiritual healing is being discussed and practiced.

It looks as if within the next half century or so, *materia medica* will have found a remedy for almost every physical disease now known, and there will then be little need of metaphysical practitioners as far as the healing of physical disease is concerned. That, however, will not solve life's problems; it will not solve the problems of the world because the world's problem is not really a problem of disease. Disease is only one of the many facets of inharmony and discord in life. Advances in medicine will not eliminate the need for spiritual healing because, even with 100 per cent success in physical healing, I do not believe that such healing will ever succeed in revealing man's Soul to him. That will be the function of the practitioner of spiritual healing. Man will find that even when all physical, mental, moral, or financial discords have been eliminated there will still be an inner unrest. Man will still not be at peace with himself.

No one will ever be completely whole until he finds himself at home in God. No one is going to be wholly satisfied even with good economic conditions until he finds his inner communion with God. Watching television will not satisfy man's Soul. Watching baseball games and football games is not the way to find peace of mind or peace of Soul, nor yet a satisfactory method of bringing peace on earth and good will to men. There is nothing wrong, nothing evil, about these things—they are all good in their place; they all have their function—but no one has ever found permanent harmony in a football game or a baseball game, in a television set, or in dancing.

The harmony of man's being is achieved only when he finds God, when he arrives at an inner communion with that which is greater than himself. That is the real healing and the lasting healing. That is the healing which the world seeks. And so it is that even were you healed of every physical or mental ill at this moment, even if your economic situation or personal relationships were entirely to your satisfaction, there would still be an unrest within, and a discontent. Regardless of how much happiness you might find in your family, you would retire at night and be alone, because there is a Something within each of us that longs to go home, that longs to live with his Father-Mother.

Spiritual healing is sought by different people for different reasons. Some seek it because of physical illness, or because of mental, moral, or financial problems; others because of an internal unrest that gives them no peace regardless of how much outer satisfaction and success they may have found. But sooner or later the realization dawns that until one establishes conscious contact with the Source of his existence, there will be unhappiness, dissatisfaction, incompleteness, regardless of how much health or wealth is his lot.

Spiritual healing is much more than a purely physical experience or even a mental experience: Healing is finding an inner communion with something greater, far greater, than anything in the world; it is finding ourselves in God, finding ourselves in a spiritual peace, an inner peace, an inner glow, all of which comes to us with the realization of God with us, the presence and power of God felt. Resting in that peace, the body resumes its normal functions, and those functions are carried on by a power not our own. The body, then, begins to show forth perfect, complete health, youth, vitality, and strength, all the gift from the Lord.

Spiritual healing is the touch of the Spirit of God in man's Soul; and when that touches him, it awakens him to a new dimension of life, a spiritual dimension: "Where the Spirit of the Lord is, there is liberty"—not that the Spirit of the Lord acts as a medicine, not that the Spirit of the Lord acts as an electrical application or as surgery, but because the Spirit of the Lord lifts the seeker into a new consciousness of life, the state of consciousness which the Master described as "My kingdom" which is not of "this world." When man attains that state of consciousness, he lives in a dimension of life other than the three-dimensional one, and he has experiences totally unknown on the human level of life. That is the goal which the world is seeking, even though it does not realize quite what that goal is or how to attain it.

Jesus gave us a glimpse of this higher dimension of life when he said to the impotent man, "Wilt thou be made whole? . . . Rise, take up thy bed, and walk," clearly indicating that God was not going to cure a physical disease, but that physical disease actually was not a power or a limiting influence; and therefore, nothing could hinder him in spite of what he was experiencing as physical discomfort. When the man responded, it meant that he was lifted into a new dimension of consciousness, one in which his physical limitations did not operate.

When my first spiritual experience came to me, I was not seeking healing as such. True, I did need healing—the healing of a cold—but in the days, weeks, months, and years preceding that day, healing had not been the object of my study and search. I did not know what it was that I was seeking and assumed that my mother was right when she told me that I was looking for God. On the particular day when this experience occurred, although I was expecting a healing and received it, the motivating force within me was not healing: It was to find God.

The strange thing, however, was that within thirty-six hours a buyer who was a customer of mine told me that if I would pray for her, she could be healed. The only prayer I knew at that time was, "Now I lay me down to sleep . . ." and it seemed obvious that that was not going to do much healing.

But she insisted that if I would pray for her, she would get well, and there was nothing for me to do but to pray. I am happy to say that I have always been honest with God, so I closed my eyes and said, "Father, you know that I don't know how to pray, and I certainly know nothing about healing. So if there is anything I should know, tell me." Very, very clearly, as much so as if a voice were speaking, I heard, "Man is not a healer." That satisfied me and that was the extent of my praying, but it was enough: The woman had her healing.

The very next day, a traveling salesman came in and said, "Joel, I don't know what your religion is, but I do know this: If you would pray for me, I could get well." What was there for me to do in such a situation? Argue? No, all

I could do was to say, "Let's close our eyes and pray."

But while my eyes were closed and apparently nothing was happening, he touched me and said, "Wonderful! The pain is all gone."

That kind of thing was a daily experience, so that I should not have been surprised when one morning about eighteen months later, as I came into my office, my business associate said to me, "You've had twenty-two telephone calls, and not one is from a customer. All these calls are from people asking you to pray for them. They want to be healed! Why don't you wake up?" With that, I left, went up town, and rented an office to engage in the practice of spiritual healing —and I have been at it ever since.

It was only after years of study, experimentation, practice, and more revelation that the answer came as to how spiritual healing is accomplished. This revelation was so different from what was being taught that I found it very hard to teach others and found very few who could understand what I was trying to say. I still have the same difficulty because spiritual healing is so strange, so revolutionary, so different from the ordinary way of thinking that it makes imparting or teaching it a difficult matter.

There is no denying the fact that it is not easy for some people, often exceedingly intelligent people, to grasp the mystery of spiritual healing. Some years ago, I was called to a hotel where a woman was dying. Her family had no knowledge or faith in metaphysics; but when they were told that there was no hope of effecting a cure through medical aid, they were willing to try metaphysical treatment as a last resort. After I had sat with the patient for a little while, I went down into the lobby where some members of the family were waiting for me. One of the men asked if I would join them for a few moments, to which I assented, thinking they wanted me to comfort them.

The conversation began with this categorical statement, "Of course, we know that we can't really expect any help in this direction because it is a well-known fact that diseases of this nature cannot be healed." When I did not respond to his comment, he continued, "Don't you agree with me?"

My reply then was, "Don't you think before we talk about that, we ought to speak for at least five minutes about the Copernican theory and dispose of that first?"

He looked at me in astonishment, "The Copernican theory? What's that? What does that have to do with it? What is it?"

"You haven't heard about it?"

"No, I don't know anything about that."

"You don't?"

"No, I can't discuss that. I haven't the faintest notion what it's all about. I don't know anything about it."

"But why should that stop you from talking about it? You don't know anything about spiritual healing as related to the healing of this disease, either, and yet you feel competent and ready to talk about that."

Such an attitude toward spiritual healing is typical of many people who find this whole subject so intangible and contrary to human reason that it is completely incomprehensible to them. They find spiritual healing difficult to understand, and to the human mind it seems foolish because all the evidence in the world is to the contrary. There is only one way that anybody will ever be able to accept the principles on which spiritual healing rests, and that is, if within his own being he feels an assurance and then begins to watch the harmony as it unfolds in his experience.

If and when you do experience any measure of healing by spiritual means, it should be clear to you that the way lies open before you to receive complete healing of mind, body, and soul. The very moment that you are an instrument through which somebody else receives healing, even of so simple a thing as indigestion or an ordinary headache, that must be the proof to you that there is a Presence, a Power; there is Something available above that which is known to the human mind. From then on it means that your work and my work must be to continue in our search and to develop ourselves in the practice of the Presence, until realization comes, followed by demonstration.

When the Wright brothers were able to keep their plane aloft for a mere fifty-seven seconds, they set the seal on transportation for all time. It was inevitable that eventually we would be able to travel as we now do at 300, 400, 1000 miles an hour. In fact there seems to be no limit to the speed which man can attain. When the first automobile successfully traveled a block, it set the seal for all time on that type of transportation, and the era of horses and carriages came to an end.

So it is when you have the experience of one first conscious realization of a transcendental Presence and Power, of that Something which we call God, Spirit, the Christ, that sets the seal forever in your mind, and you know that one of these days, whether it is accomplished slowly or rapidly, you are going to be able to say with Paul, "I live; yet not I, but Christ liveth in me," or with Jesus, "I can of mine own self do nothing . . . the Father that dwelleth in me, he doeth the works."

It is not of too much importance whether you or I have fewer or more problems during our threescore years and ten, twenty, or thirty. It is of tremendous importance to the world, however, because insofar as one individual can show forth a measure of health, harmony, inner peace, joy, satisfaction, and abundance sufficient unto his needs, in that degree, is that person the light of the world, the inspiration for others to follow, the light which fills them with that same hope, that same ambition, and that same willingness to sacrifice just a few hours a day to the end that they also may know God. And so spiritual healing becomes embodied in consciousness through a light here and a light there.

Sometimes we are likely to forget what an influence the life of one man or one woman can be. Not one of us knows the tremendous significance of some particular moment of our lives—any given moment or any given hour. There are people who have had an experience similar to that which I had late in 1928 when, while in meditation with one who was truly illumined, the Spirit descended upon me, and I was lifted out of what we might call "this world." After that the things of this world no longer attracted me, and from then on my whole life was lived in my inner being with the Bible, with metaphysical and mystical writings, and in the company of those on the spiritual path. All the rest of my life dropped away.

Those two hours changed the entire course of my life because when I left I had received the illumination that took me out of the business world and into the spiritual healing ministry, which has resulted in a continuity of unfoldment from that moment to this. Who could put a value on that visit? Who could put a value on that day? There is no way of measuring the value of the priceless.

But that experience could not have come to me except for the thirteen preceding years spent in reading the Bible and metaphysical books, begging and pleading with God, "Please, God, please, speak to me! Say something to me. Do something to let me know there is a God." Every bit of that search prepared me for that one minute which changed my entire life. You do not know what minute your life is going to be changed or when you may come in contact with the person, the message, or the book which may open your Soul. If by any chance you think that you are too unimportant or too insignificant a person, just remember a few of those who are inspiring this generation and others to come. Think of what a limitless influence the health and harmony of your life may also prove to be when it becomes known that you attained this wholeness through your devotion to God, through thinking, pondering, and loving God.

The ultimate salvation of the world through spiritual healing will come through an individual *you* and an individual *me*, through an individual *him* and an individual *her*, here and there, who show forth by the fruitage in their lives something which causes a friend or a relative to seek spiritual understanding and which ultimately encourages the neighbor down the street also to "go and do likewise."

Each one is a thread in this skein, in this rope—a link in the chain. Each one is a beam in the whole light. No one can ever be more than that. It takes one person here, another there, each contributing his part, to make up the whole. Every time a healing is brought about, whether for yourself or for another, the world benefits. The world is that much closer to receiving the full spiritual light because of each individual healing that takes place.

The secret of healing must inevitably be learned: first, that God is; and second, that the nature of God is good—the nature of God is love, the nature of God is wisdom, and the function of God is not only to create an image after His own likeness, but to maintain and sustain that image, including all mankind, in a divine embrace of harmony, wholeness, completeness, and perfection. That is the truth about God, but that truth does not necessarily mean that you or I will benefit by God's infinite, creative, maintaining, and sustaining being and nature, because there is yet something for us to do. That something is: "Ye shall know the truth, and the truth shall make you free."

God's work is done. God's work was done in the beginning. Two times two is already four, but the truth of that statement only becomes functional in your experience in proportion to your awareness of that principle. The telegraph, telephone, airplane, radio, and color television were possible millions of years ago. The *principles* of every ancient and modern invention have always existed. They only awaited a Samuel F. B. Morse, a Thomas A. Edison, a Charles F. Kettering, a Guglielmo Marconi, a Glenn Curtiss and Orville Wright, an Enrico Fermi, or an Albert Einstein to come along and *reveal* the principles governing these revolutionary ideas.

All the music, all the art, and all the literature exist already

—all that has ever been known, all that is known now, and all that will be known, composed, and written for the next million years already exists. All of these have existed from the beginning. It becomes necessary for us to learn how to turn to that spiritual realm within and let God's creation, that which has always existed, come forth.

God's work is done, finished and complete, but it is unfolding to our conscious awareness in proportion as we learn the truth and how to bring ourselves into harmony with that truth. The next step is not up to God; it is up to you and to me.

CHAPTER II

IS GOD A SERVANT?

To most people God is still the great "Unknown," ignorantly worshiped. How few people there are who have sought to understand the nature of God, who have ever asked themselves: "Is there a God? How do I know there is a God? I have been told that there is a God, people say there is a God, and I have read books about God; but if I had to go on a witness stand and take an oath that I know there is a God, what would my answer be? Could I swear that I really do know that there is a God? What evidence do I have? Have I seen God face to face? Have I felt God within me?"

How would you answer such questions? Would you say, "Yes, I know there is a God, and this is what He is like?" How would you describe God? Can He be described? He is not like what most men think Him to be. He is nothing like anything you can imagine, or anything you can think, because any idea of God that you entertain with your mind must be finite; any idea of God you may have, you have created within yourself or learned from someone else.

Stop and think for a moment where your ideas of God have come from. Who gave them to you? Is it not true that you, yourself, either made up your ideas or concept of God, or you read something and accepted some version of what someone else believed, or you have been taught from infancy to accept someone else's concept of God? Are your ideas of God man-made or are they the result of inner experience?

21

To Jesus, who had realized his complete oneness with God, God meant "Father"—"the Father within." However, for us to think of God as Father is immediately to think in terms of some particular concept of a father. Each of us has a different concept of father—the result of his own experience. In this modern age, children often consider their parents as some kind of a servant born to do their will, and many adults have simply incorporated this concept of parents as servants into their concept of God and have made a God for themselves in the image and likeness of these childhood concepts. They think of God as a superhuman being just waiting for the privilege of granting them favors, of some kind of a God whose favor can be secured in one way or another, and that if the right combination of words can be learned, a person can even get God's favor to the extent of persuading God to do healing work for him. There is no such God. You do not need God's favor any more than you need man's favor. All of God's favor you will ever need, you already have.

If you will turn within and acknowledge that you do not know what Jesus meant when he referred to God as Father, and then wait for God to tell you what God is as Father, you may have an experience similar to mine, although probably not exactly the same because each one receives God's wisdom in a different way. When I turned within and asked, "What is God as Father?" the answer came, "Creative Principle." God is the Creative Principle of this universe, and Its[1] nature is an infinite, all-embracing love.

The nature of God is such that what God is not already doing God cannot do and could not be induced to do. Understand that clearly. What God is not doing now, it would be a waste of time asking or expecting Him to do: No one

[1] In the spiritual literature of the world, the varying concepts of God are indicated by the use of such words as "Father," "Mother," "Soul," "Spirit," "Principle," "Love," "Life." Therefore, in this book the author has used the pronouns "He" and "It," or "Himself" and "Itself," interchangeably in referring to God.

prays to God for the sun to rise in the morning or to set at night; no one prays to God to arrange the incoming and outgoing tides; no one prays to God to have roses come from roses, or pineapples from pineapples, or butter from milk; no one prays to God to change the laws of automotive engineering or airplane dynamics. In short, most people seem perfectly willing to let God run His own universe in His own way until their own little selves become involved. Then they turn to God and say, "O God, won't you do this for me? Won't you protect me or mine? Won't you heal me or mine? Won't you send food and clothing to me and mine?"

Of course God does not answer such a prayer. God has provided more food in the earth and in the sea than all the people on the face of the earth can consume. It is futile to pray to God for more. God's work was done in the beginning, and He found it good. It is useless to try to get God to change His universe for your benefit or mine, for your nation or mine, or for your family or mine. If you want to experience the grace of God, it is necessary to align yourself with God and receive the grace of God as it is now flowing, always has, and always will.

What is needed is to know Him aright, and that you do through contemplating truth. As you dwell in meditation[2] upon the nature of God, very quickly you will find that the nature of God is love and intelligence. The intelligent, loving nature of God is your assurance that you will have a crop of roses from the rose seedlings you have planted in the fertile ground, and not something that you do not want.

In the midst of such contemplation, it will dawn, "What have I to fear? There is a God and that God is love. That ends my whole problem. If God were not love, then I really would have a problem; but the minute I know that God is love, I have no more problems. That ends them. If I know

[2] See the author's *The Art of Meditation* (New York: Harper & Brothers, 1956; London: George Allen and Unwin, 1956).

that God is infinite intelligence and that it is His good pleasure to give me the kingdom, what kind of a problem can I have? I can forget anything that looked like a problem and begin to help the men, women, and children who do not know that God is love, help those who have heard the words but do not believe them; and in helping them, I bring the conscious realization home to myself."

As you meditate upon the nature of God, you will perceive that there never has been a time when God did not exist, and even from the limited standpoint of human reason that would indicate that there never will be a time when God will cease to exist. With that conviction comes the revelation that God is eternal. Furthermore, there is no place where God is not. The findings of astronomy demonstrate how infinite is God's creation of sun, stars, moons, and planets, and also with what intelligent direction and order they move, each in its own orbit. The natural deduction of such cogitation is the realization, "If it is true that all that the Father has is mine, then the Father-qualities are the qualities of my individual being. The same wisdom, law, and order operate in my experience. All that constitutes the nature and character of God constitutes the nature of my individual being and of yours."

Since it is true that God is the same yesterday, today, and forever, then God cannot do anything today that God was not doing yesterday or that God will not be doing tomorrow. God does not have health to give; God does not have harmony to give, or wealth, or employment. Because God is love, God cannot withhold health, harmony, or peace. What kind of a God would let you be sick until you got around to praying to Him? Such a God is merely a glorified human being and not God at all. God is a God of omnipotence, omnipresence, omniscience, and God knows your needs before you do. It is His pleasure to give you the kingdom and to give it without your sitting around, waiting, trying to find out how you are going to influence Him in your behalf. Yet, is not that what the world is doing? Are not people spending their time trying to find ways to influence God to do something for them?

Unless you understand the nature of God as one infinite Good, you will be attempting to use God to gain your own ends; you will be attempting to use Truth. Be willing to be used *by* God; be willing to be used *by* Truth. Be willing to be an instrument through which Truth reveals Itself, but do not attempt to *use* God. Never try to use God, Truth.

If you understood the nature of God, never would you pray to God for any *thing*. God has only the gift of Himself to give, and in that gift all needs are met. Any other kind of God is a man-made myth, invented by the pagans centuries before the Master. The pagans worshiped that kind of a God; they worshiped many gods, always for the purpose of *getting* something from God. When there was no rain, they prayed for rain; when there was too much rain, they prayed to have it cease; when there were floods or storms, they prayed to have God stop them; and when there was no food, they prayed to God for food. Prayer such as that is purely paganistic, a relic from the days when people made a God after their own image because they had no idea at all of what God is. Since they could not get all they wanted from one God, they made many gods: From one they got rain; crops from another; fertility from another; and something else from another.

When Abraham came with a teaching of one God, the only innovation as far as his followers were concerned was that, instead of praying to ten gods for ten things, they prayed to one God for the same ten things. They prayed to a God who rewarded them when they were good, a God who punished them when they were evil.

God is not like that. The nature of God is such that His rain falls on the just and on the unjust. He is equally available to the saint and to the sinner. He looks impartially upon all regardless of color, race, creed, religion, or lack of religion.

The difference in people's experience does not lie with God; it lies in their ignorance or lack of awareness of God.

To pray to God for things—health, money, houses, companionship—would be to look upon Him as a servant whom you can command to obey your wish. Do you really believe that God is an instrument made for your pleasure, or are you made for His pleasure? Do you really believe that God, whether in the heavens or within you, is just awaiting your call to serve your purpose, to gratify your desires? Or is God the spiritual creative Principle of the universe whom this universe serves and whose purpose you serve?

The world is riding horseback to hell waiting for God to serve it, instead of humbly realizing that you and I, just the same as the sun, the moon, and the stars, the birds, the animals, and the fish were made to serve God's purpose. The image and likeness of God, the very God-Self expressed, was made to serve Its purpose, to glorify God, not man. God is not meant to glorify man: Man is meant to glorify God. Reverse the usual concept of God as something or other that you can instruct or advise, and bring to light in your consciousness the fact that you are to be taught of God.

Be receptive and responsive to the divine Impulse from within, that Truth may use you to reveal Its glory. The heavens show forth God's glory; the earth shows forth His glory in multitudinous ways; and you show forth God's glory. You show forth God's glory—not your own glory. You do not express God; you do not reflect God. No, God expresses God, and that expression appears as you. God reflects Himself into this universe as you, but you have nothing to do with it. God expresses Himself; God shows forth His own handiwork; God glorifies not you or me: God glorifies Himself. The nearer you approach to that vision, the greater is the glory of God that is being shown forth by you.

Every knee must bend; every head must bow to God. "In all thy ways acknowledge him, and he shall direct thy paths" —not in all thy ways tell Him your desires or tell Him how virtuous you are, or how virtuous your family, your community, or nation is. *No, tell God nothing. Acknowledge God!* How else can you acknowledge God except to realize:

God, Thou art the infinite Intelligence which hast created this entire universe, the Intelligence that knows how to govern it without any help from me. Forgive me, Father, if I have ever told Thee what I need or what my family or nation needs. Father, forgive me every time that I have lifted my eyes in the hope that Thou wouldst serve me. Let me understand that I was created in Thy image and likeness to show forth Thy glory. The heavens declare the glory of God; the earth shows forth His bounty.[3]

Man, the highest creation, should show forth God to the fullest extent. Man, individual you and I, should show forth immortality, eternality, infinity, all good, health, harmony, wholeness, infinite abundance—not yours or mine, but His. His grace should be evident in your eyes. The harmony of His body should be made manifest as the health of your body and mine. The infinite wealth, the infinite abundance of God, should be expressed in your individual purse and household, not by any virtue of yours, not because you are good and deserve it, but because God is love, and the nature of love is that you bear fruit richly. It is God's great pleasure to give you the kingdom, not to have you sweat for it, labor for it, earn it, or even deserve it. Your good should come to you, not by the sweat of your brow, but by a divine grace operating in you—a grace which you prevent by trying to make God your servant instead of making of yourself a servant of God.

[3] The italicized portions of this book are spontaneous meditations which have come to the author during periods of uplifted consciousness and are not in any sense intended to be used as affirmations, denials, or formulas. They have been inserted in this book from time to time to serve as examples of the free flowing of the Spirit. As the reader practices the Presence, he, too, in his exalted moments, will receive ever new and fresh inspiration as the outpouring of the Spirit.

Gradually your concept of God will change, and when it does, you will stop praying to a Santa Claus God. You do not give up praying, but prayer now begins to have a new meaning for you. You begin to see that God cannot give and God cannot withhold. You can shut yourself off from the grace of God, but through prayer, you can be reunited with your Source. Your prayer will not be an asking or a seeking for any *thing*; it will be an asking and a seeking and a knocking for more light, greater spiritual wisdom, greater discernment.

Gladly will you give up everything, if only it will bring you one step closer to the realization of your true relationship with God, which is that of a child of God, heir of God, the very expression of God's own infinite being. God's being becomes your being; God's wisdom becomes your wisdom; God's life becomes your immortal life; and your body becomes the temple of the living God. God's strength, youth, and vitality flow through you.

God is the infinity of good, always about God's business of unfolding, disclosing, and revealing Himself as this universe. God cannot add to that and God has never subtracted from that. God can never increase; God can never decrease. *God is.* Five thousand years ago, this was true—*God is.* A thousand years from now—*God is.* A million years from now —*God is.* To say that God is infinite or God is good or God is life or God is love is to say no more than that God is. That is the limit of our knowledge about God—*God is*:

If God is, then I am. I cannot say, "I am yesterday," and I cannot say, "I am tomorrow." All I can say is, "If God is, I am." I seek nothing, for all that the Father has is mine; all that God is, I am. God has made me in His image and likeness and has given me full possession and dominion over everything that exists in the heavens, in the air, on the earth, and in the waters beneath the earth. God has given me dominion. What power is there, then, that can harm me? Since I have been blessed with God-given dominion, there

*are no powers that can enter me that "defileth or maketh a
lie."*

Knowing that God is, makes it unnecessary for you to find
some God-power to do something for you. God is, and God
is *is-ing*. God is always *is-ing*. There is no such thing as God
was-ing! There is only God being God all the time. That is
our salvation—God is always being God; God is always
being power; God is always being love; God is always being
life; God is always being wisdom. Try to understand God in
this light of *is*—not was two thousand years ago, not will
be if we deserve it.

Go out into a park where fresh grass is growing, or where
the leaves are sprouting on the trees, or a little later when
the blossoms are bursting. Notice how God is *is-ing* every
single minute as leaves, flowers, and fruit. And the miracle
is that nobody is praying for it; nobody is asking for it;
nobody is telling God how much he needs these things—
the fruit and vegetables and cattle on a thousand hills. And
yet in spite of that, God is attending to all of it.

Yes, God is attending to all our needs without assistance
or interference from any of us. There may be some readers
who remember that in the early 1900's the American public
was warned of the great danger which lay just ahead because
not enough horses were being bred: "In a few years there
will not be enough horses in this country to take care of the
commercial needs of the country. Americans, do something
about it." The answer to this call to action might well have
been, "Why not pray?" But in a few years, there was no
longer a need for horses because man's ingenuity had de-
vised the internal combustion engine, and its use in automobiles, trucks, and tractors replaced horses. And what would
we have been praying for? Horses? Do you not see the
foolishness of believing that man can prepare for the future
or that his wisdom is sufficient to provide for the future?
God's grace is our sufficiency in all things—today, tomorrow,

and a thousand years from now. God is about God's business. God is expressing Itself now, and the highest form of prayer is, "God already is." Be satisfied that God *is*; be satisfied that God is omnipresent, omnipotent; be satisfied that God is where you are this instant.

Until the moment of illumination comes, when you behold Him as He is, be satisfied to know the nature of God. As you understand God as the creative Principle of life, that which maintains and sustains all creation, that which is the intelligence of this universe, the very love and life and fiber of this universe, you will not pray to It: You will rejoice in It, and that will be your prayer. You will commune with It, seeking nothing for yourself, seeking nothing for anyone else, and never relegating God to the role of a servant meant to do your will or to satisfy your desires.

God satisfies His own infinite nature in creating, maintaining, and sustaining this grand and glorious universe, and those of us who are in it are the servants of the most High. Do not expect God to serve man. Understand man's function to be the servant of God, the glorifier of God, showing forth all that God is on this earth. Change the nature of your prayer so that you are not trying to get a great big God to do a little tiny "you" a favor.

Too many people act as if they really believed that they could direct God and expect Him to fulfill their desires. They must understand that they are here to be the instruments through which God appears on earth. Instead of letting God speak to them, too many people speak to God, tell Him, ask, direct, even command God; and that is why there is no response. The response only comes when they can be like Moses who heard the voice of God, and the voice of God directed him, told him what to do and how to do it.

As slaves under Pharaoh, the Hebrews endured many hardships during their captivity. They believed they were worshiping the one God, and because of their faith they were taunted by the soldiers of Pharaoh, "What good is your one God? What does your God do for you? You are still slaves of us Egyptians; you still suffer under the Pharaoh. Where is this God? What does this God do?"

For countless years, their only answer must have been, "This one great God does nothing for us but let us live and die in slavery." And so it was until one among them, in humility, opened himself to God.

Moses waited a long time for God to speak to him, and you will find that you may have to wait a long time, too. But after you once hear the still small voice, it comes more frequently and then eventually it comes at will: You have only to close your eyes, wait a second, and whatever is necessary comes into your conscious awareness. From the moment that Moses made himself a servant of God, he was God-led, God-directed, God-sustained, God-fed; and then, through Moses, God could act to save the Hebrew people.

People of any nation can be saved, of any race, of any family, if they have learned to pray and to open themselves so that the Voice can speak within them—direct them, lead them, guide them, feed them, clothe them, house them:

Here I am, Father, listening for Your voice. My inner ears are open. I have no requests, no demands, no hopes, no ambitions. I do not ask You to do anything You are not already doing. I await Your word of grace. I am the servant of the most High.

Be willing to be a servant of the most High. Stand on the *Is-ness* of God. Pray in confidence; pray in the faith that when the finger of the Lord touches you, nothing shall enter that in any wise "defileth or maketh a lie." When the finger of the Lord is upon you, you live, move, and have your being under the grace of God—not under the law. Those who look to you for leadership will be led out of their slavery to disease, out of their fear of lack, and out of their bondage to persons and conditions.

CHAPTER III

ONE POWER

To understand the nature of God is to understand the basic principle of spiritual healing. Is it the nature of God to heal disease? Do you really believe that? If God is all-powerful and all-loving, why did He not heal it yesterday? Why is He waiting for today? And why is He not doing it today? Most of the people in the world believe that God works through doctors to heal them, but according to statistics, God was not doing too satisfactory a job of that before this century, was He? One hundred years ago, people were dying daily of diseases which today are healed in twenty-four hours. Why? Did God want them to die, but not us? Is God a respecter of persons?

God never has had pleasure in our dying; God never will have pleasure in our dying; and, furthermore, God has never been responsible for our dying. People died because medical science had not advanced to the stage where their doctors knew enough to keep them alive, and some, in this last century, because their metaphysical and spiritual practitioners did not know enough to keep them alive. When you think of such things, the question inevitably arises, "Does God have anything to do with a person's being diseased? What does God have to do with healing him? There must be another principle involved in healing. And what is it?"

That principle is revealed through an understanding of the nature of God and the nature of that with which you are dealing. When you understand God to be infinite love, infinite wisdom, and infinite good, you will know that God is "of purer eyes than to behold evil, and canst not look on iniquity." Disease is man-created, and only through man's developed spiritual consciousness will it be eradicated.

If you can grasp the significance and truth of that statement, you will realize, "Then the development of this spiritual consciousness is my responsibility," and you will be correct. Through prayer and contemplation, let the nature of God be revealed. Discover for yourself that God has never empowered a disease to kill; God has never ordained a disease to destroy; and because of the all-loving nature of God, disease must be outside the creative, maintaining, and sustaining power of God, which means that it is without cause, without foundation, law, substance, or action.

There is only one power, and that one is God. The realization of God as one power, however, does not mean that God is a power *over* something. The belief that God is a power over something stems from our interpretation of the word "power." God is power. That is true, but in order to understand God as power, it becomes necessary to change our concept of the meaning of the word "power." The word itself connotes something which can be used, like the power of electricity, the power of heat, or the power of cold, all of which can be utilized for some purpose. Wind is another example of power which can be harnessed or used. But is God that kind of a power?

One power means what it says—one power, and it leaves no room for any other powers over which that one power is to be exercised, to be used or applied. God never can be used, and yet God is power; in fact, God is not only power, but the only power in this spiritual universe.

To illustrate: Under any and all conditions, do, re, and mi have certain values. Do is always do; re is always re; mi is always mi. They may be sung off key by the whole world, but that does not change the value of do, re, or mi in the harmonic scale. So it is with numbers: 1, 2, 3, 4, and 5 are complete within themselves wherever used, or in whatever language. What established that as an invariable law? Not you and certainly not I—not any man.

There is a principle of life that has given to numbers and to musical notes their values. There is a principle of life that expresses itself in complete and perfect tones of music, complete and perfect numbers, complete and perfect laws of the universe. Who established these principles? Who maintains them? Who, but God—God who is the power of this universe, the creative and maintaining and sustaining principle of this universe?

Can you use that God-power? No, but you can bring yourself into accord *with* that power. You can bring yourself under the reign or government of that power, but you cannot use it. You cannot move a single star in heaven. You cannot change the tides: The hour of their coming and going is set for a thousand years ahead.

God is not a great power which will do something to the negative powers of sin, disease, lack, and limitation, if you can contact Him. God is power only in the sense that God is the creative principle of this universe. God has given us the sun for certain purposes, the oceans, and the tides. God has given us the land, the valleys, the mountains, and the woods. All this God has given us, but He has not given us the power to use Him for our purposes. The gifts of God can be used, but the power of God cannot be used. God is one power, maintaining and sustaining His universe eternally, immortally, perfectly, harmoniously, and justly.

When you begin to live from the standpoint of one power, the entire tenor of your experience is changed. In the world, you are constantly confronted with the appearance of persons, places, or things of a destructive nature: There is always something which would attempt to destroy your peace, your health, or the harmony of your affairs. The spiritually illumined of all ages have learned that these things are not power except insofar as they are given power by accepting them as powers, and then fearing and fighting them.

The Master, Christ Jesus, had no fear of any earthly power because he knew that there is only one power. When his disciples boasted of their power over evil, his rebuke was quick, "Rejoice not, that the spirits are subject unto you; but rather rejoice, because your names are written in heaven." In other words, he was telling them to rejoice because they had learned the great secret, the great revelation: There is but one power—God. Therefore, there was no evil to be subject unto them, not even in His name. This is the secret that is not known to the materialistic world, to the mental, or even to some in the religious world. This is the secret known only to the mystical world: God is infinite power, and besides God there is no other power.

Is there power then in sin, disease, lack, limitation, death, weather, climate, infection, or contagion? Go back over it again: *God is infinite power*. Then, can there be power in infection and contagion? Can there be power in weather or climate? Can there be power in sin, disease, lack, limitation, or death? Can there be, if God is the only power?

If it is true that God is one, the only law there can be is the law of God. Is there a law of disease if God is infinite law? The nature of God as one eliminates any such possibility; it eliminates laws of disease, laws of sin, laws of false appetite. If there is any law on earth, it must be the law of God; and since God is infinite, God's law must partake of the nature of God. And what is that nature but love, intelligence, and wisdom? God is love, infinite love. Can there then be any power in hate, jealousy, animosity? Can there be power in anything that is not of the nature of love?

All evidence points to God as the infinite Intelligence of this universe. Is there any power other than that infinite, loving Intelligence? If not, why then should you fear a law of disease, an injury to the brain, or the movement of the stars? Why should you fear anything in heaven or on earth or in the waters beneath the earth? If there is but one power operating, then nothing else is power.

As soon as you begin to understand the nature of God as one—one life, one being, one law, one cause—immediately is brought to your attention evidence which would contradict that oneness. The world points out all the material laws which appear to exist as against the one spiritual law—disease as against the one spiritual life, age and death as against eternality and immortality—but if you understand God as one, you will perceive that in the infinite nature of God, there could be no power to oppose God. There is nothing negative in God's nature. As you perceive the nature of God to be a continuous state of immortal, eternal, harmonious being, you will discover that all these so-called forces and powers of the world are not power. Then you will understand what the Master meant when he said, "Resist not evil."

When this reveals itself to you, never again will you appeal to God to overcome error in any form; never will you turn to truth to overcome error; never will you use right thinking to offset wrong thinking; never will you pray to God to heal disease, sin, or fear: You will know that in the infinite nature of God's goodness, disease, sin, and fear do not exist as power. In God's kingdom, there is no such thing as truth *over* error, God *over* the devil, good *over* evil, right *over* wrong, or Spirit *over* matter: *There is only infinite, immortal, eternal God-being.*

If you can be made to fight or to look to God to overcome some form of activity, you will lose. In fact, if you can be made to look to God to overcome anything on earth, you will lose. Only in proportion as you realize that "as in heaven, so on earth," God is infinite, and that the battle is not yours—only in the attaining of that consciousness—can you come into harmony.

The moment that you can be tempted to fight a person, a sin, or a disease, you become engaged in a battle which in the end will destroy you. In and of itself, a problem has no power; but by imputing power to it, you then begin to react as if it had power. If you try to meet your problem by means of whatever you accept as material power, there will always be the possibility that the opponent, whether that opponent be a person, thing, or a condition, will prove to have a stronger belief in material power than your own power. If you try to meet the problem by means of mental might or right thinking, again there is the possibility that your opponent will wield a stronger mental weapon.

A drastic change must take place in individual consciousness to enable the people of this world to cope with life and all its problems and to look at evil—sin, disease, war, poverty—and be able to say, "What is that to me? Thou couldest have no power over me unless it came from the creative Principle of the universe which is God. I am resting in one power."

Until you can realize that there is nothing to battle because there is only one power, you will be carrying a chip on your shoulders, everlastingly fighting people, sin, disease, false appetite, lonesomeness, and poverty. One condition after another will arise in your experience as long as you are fighting and resisting; but when you understand God as one power, you become convinced that there is nothing to oppose Him.

The only way this can be proved, when the appearance of sin, disease, death, lack, or limitation touches you, whether in your own experience or in that of your friends or relatives, is to sit in an inner stillness and realize that God is infinite. Wait in quietness and in peace until an inner assurance comes, "There are no gods besides Me, no other powers, nothing for you to fear. Thou art my beloved child."

This is spiritual wisdom: There is nothing with which to contend, nothing to heal or reform or supply or overcome. Know the truth:

There is only one God—one God, whether in the Occident or in the Orient; one God, whether among the Greeks or the Jews, the bond or the free. There is only one God, and the I in the midst of me is that God—infinite, omnipresent, omnipotent, omniscient, the only power.

There is no power besides the I that I am. That I that I am is immortal and eternal. Because of my oneness with the Father—my oneness with the I that I am—all the intelligence, all the wisdom, all the life, all the spirituality, all the power, all the good, and all the grace of God are embodied within me.

To do spiritual healing it is necessary to be able to look any form of sin or disease in the face with complete confidence, "Neither do I fear thee, nor will I battle thee. Why should I fear what mortal man can do to me? Why should I fear what mortal things or persons or conditions can do to me, if God Himself is the only law, presence, power, cause, substance, and reality? I will stand still and see the salvation of the Lord."

Our devotion is to a God so infinite that besides Him nothing exists to be wiped out or destroyed. Nothing exists which has power to limit, to hinder, or to prevent anyone who understands the principle from carrying on any rightful activity, since God in the midst of him is an all-knowing intelligence, a divine love, an infinity of power, the only creative influence or principle in the entire universe.

In this principle is embodied not only the secret of healing but the secret of harmony in your life; you are now carried through life rhythmically, as on a beam of light. All that is required of you, He performs, that *He* at the center of your being, that Infinite Invisible that works while you sleep, that Infinite Invisible that goes before you and prepares the place for you, making those you meet along the way receptive and responsive to the love you express.

After persistent practice of this principle, you come to see that it is literally true: God is the infinity of being, the allness of being, and all the things the world is battling are not power at all. In moments of illumination, you look out on the world and behold world appearances dissolving as darkness dissolves before the light. In those exalted moments, you can invite all the lions and tigers of the world into your consciousness, knowing that the light that is there will dissolve the appearance and reveal them in their true nature.

CHAPTER IV

THE LANGUAGE OF SPIRITUAL HEALING

Not long ago I talked with an orthodox minister who
had just finished reading my book, *Practicing the Presence*.[1]
He had enjoyed it very much, found it challenging; but he
added that the langauge and some of the terms used were
new to him. Certainly it is true that, to the reader untutored
in mysticism, some terms are incomprehensible; but it must
be remembered that mysticism, like every other field of
study, has its own specialized terminology.

Spiritual healing as taught in The Infinite Way is built
around a few words. Before we go on to consider these words,
let me explain briefly what The Infinite Way is: It is a
spiritual teaching consisting of principles which anyone may
follow and practice, irrespective of his religious affiliation.
The Infinite Way reveals the nature of God to be one infinite
power, intelligence, and love; the nature of individual being
to be one with His qualities and character, expressed in infinite forms and variety; and the nature of the discords of this
world to be a misconception of God's expression of Himself
in His universe. These are universal principles based on the
message of the Master, Christ Jesus, who taught that man
can realize his oneness with God through conscious communion with God, thereby bringing about peace on earth,
harmony, and wholeness.

[1] New York: Harper & Brothers, 1958; London: L. N. Fowler &
Co., Ltd., 1958.

In this new language of spiritual healing, the first and most important word that must be understood is the little word "as," an understanding of which eliminates forever all sense of duality: God is manifest *as* individual being. If God is manifest as individual being, there is not God *and* man; there is not God *and* you; therefore, there cannot be a person going to God for something.

During the years when I was devoting my time exclusively to the healing work, as patients came to me I learned not to see them as human beings, nor to look to a God to patch them up. I saw that everyone who came to me was God appearing *as* individual being, and that truth revealed harmony. That truth revealed the divinity of their being and body, and that revelation was the foundation stone of The Infinite Way.

There is only God manifesting Its infinite spiritual nature *as* your being. "I and my Father are one"—not two. In that oneness, all that God is, you are. When you understand "as," God appearing *as* individual you and me, you will understand why all that God is, you are:

"Son, thou art ever with me, and all that I have is thine." *I am joint-heir with Christ to all the heavenly riches. "I can of mine own self do nothing"—but because of my one-ness with the Father, all that God is, I am. Wherever I am, the Father within me is; therefore, wherever I am, the Father within me is about His business.*

God appearing *as* individual being—God appearing as you —is a secret of The Infinite Way; it is a secret of spiritual healing. This "you" is not a reflection or a separate idea or something *less* than God, but God, Itself, made manifest— God, the Father, appearing on earth as individual Being. Oneness is the secret.

After you have assimilated this truth by living with it, by practicing it, by looking out at every man, woman, and child, every animal, vegetable, and mineral in the world, and realizing, "This is not what it seems to be: This is God appearing *as*," you develop that healing consciousness which never looks at people and judges them by their humanhood, but which is immediately in contact with their spiritual consciousness. You train yourself to see people, not as they look, but to see through their eyes, back of their eyes, realizing that there sits the Christ of God. As you do that, you learn to ignore appearances, and instead of trying to heal or reform someone, or improve him, you are really bearing witness to his Christ-identity.

Second, and equal in importance to the word "as," is the word "is." If it is true that God manifests *as* individual being, then harmony already *is* the truth about every person. And so the great word in prayer and treatment is, "is." You are never trying to heal anyone; you are never trying to reform or enrich anyone: You live always in the realization of *Is*. Since God *is* your being, harmony *is*; since all that the Father has *is* yours, you are now in the fullness and completeness of God; since God *is* the activity of your being, harmony *is* the law of your being. By never dwelling in the past or future, you live in the consciousness of *Is*.

Even though you see a sick person, a drunken person, or a dying one, you ignore the appearance and declare, "*Is*." Because of "*as*," "*is*" must be. Do you see that? If God is appearing *as* you, then harmony *is* the truth about you.

The most powerful word in the vocabulary of prayer is the verb "is": Harmony *is*; God *is*; joy *is*; peace *is*; abundance *is*; Omnipresence *is*. In the presence of Omnipresence, is there anything to be healed, changed, reformed, overcome, or destroyed? You look at every appearance, but you do not permit yourself to become disturbed by any one of them. Your eyes may bear witness to somebody's illness, poverty, or sinfulness, but Spirit tells you, "No, this *is* God made manifest. This *is* the very incarnation of God; therefore, harmony *is* true, regardless of what my eyes see or my ears hear."

Spiritual healing demands a developed consciousness. It is

a consciousness that is able to see through the appearance, an inner vision that assures you of this truth even when the senses testify to a thief or a dying person. Nobody can be a successful spiritual healer except the person who has that inner assurance: "This is my beloved Son, in whom I am well pleased." It matters not what the outer senses may testify. Something within has to sing a song, and the song it must sing is, "This is my beloved Son, in whom I am well pleased. . . . I in the midst of you am mighty."

Words will not do that. It has to be an inner conviction, and that is only attained through practice, through realization, and finally through the grace of God which comes to you in your inner Self. When you can sit beside a very sick person with no trace of fear because something inside of you is singing, "This is my beloved Son; I in the midst of you am mighty. I will never leave you nor forsake you," then you are a spiritual healer. That takes development, brought about by practice, until the day comes when this Voice speaks to you from within. Otherwise this consciousness is received through the grace of God as a gift.

It is difficult to achieve this conviction, however, until certain other facets related to spiritual healing are clarified. One of the most important of these is the function of the mind.

In the early days of metaphysical healing, it was taught that the body is subject to the mind. This was such a novel idea, so new and challenging, that modern man began the practice of using his mind to control his body. For a short time, he found that it worked, and sometimes it still works with beginners. The fallacy in this technique, however, is that it leaves out of consideration the fact that behind thought there must be a thinker, and that the thinker is not a person: The thinker is God, the Soul of man.

The mind is an instrument of awareness. You can know the truth with the mind, but you do not create things with the mind. Even an inventor does not create with the mind.

He becomes aware of certain natural laws which have always existed and learns how to bring them together and utilize them. The right use of the mind as an instrument of awareness makes it not only a powerful instrument, but one that increases in its capacity the more it is used, continuously unfolding new potentialities.

Once it is understood that the mind is an instrument, it must also be understood of what it is the instrument, because to be an instrument there must be something governing and controlling the instrument. Unfortunately, most people have never found the Center within, which can effectively control the mind. In mental science, students who try to control the mind by will power or by changing their thoughts usually discover that the mind cannot be controlled by man and often end up in a worse condition than when they started, making nervous wrecks of themselves.

The mind is an instrument for something higher than itself. That Something is your Self, your true identity, and when It governs the mind and controls it, you will find yourself at peace—perfect peace, a peace that passeth understanding.

You will have a correct picture and a good example of the proper use of the mind, if you can recall some photographs you may have seen of Thomas A. Edison. Almost always Edison is pictured with his hand up to his ear in an attitude of intense listening. Those who worked with him in the laboratory have recounted story after story of how he would give them an experiment to work on, which they would carry out as far as they could, and then they would call upon him for assistance. Immediately, Edison's hand would go up to his ear, he would listen, and then give directions as to the next step.

Let me point out the difference between attempting to use the mind as a creative faculty and using the mind as an instrument of awareness. If I were operating on the level of mind or thought, I would close my eyes and affirm over and over again, "Your body is well; your body functions normally; your body responds to this truth that I am knowing"; and in all probability, there would be some healing and some benefit derived from such practice. As a matter of fact, in the early days of metaphysics, there were remarkable healings. Actually, however, it was never the full truth that the mind of one person could control the body either of himself or of another person. It was one of those on-the-way-to-getting-there places; it was a stopping place, a higher level than believing that the body, in and of itself, contains the issues of life.

From the standpoint of spiritual healing and spiritual living in which God is understood as the Soul, the law, and the life unto all being, and in which the mind is an instrument and the body the outer manifestation, the procedure is entirely different. If you are operating from that basis, when someone asks for help, you will close your eyes and *you will think no thoughts.* You will take no thought for what he shall eat or what he shall drink or what his health shall be. You will merely sit there, knowing that your mind is an avenue of receptivity. Receptive to what? Receptive to the still small voice, to that which is called God, that which is the Soul of man. You will make no declarations, but you will maintain a listening attitude, and then the still small voice will utter itself, and the earth will melt.

In the silence, in which you have become almost a vacuum —a listening vacuum—always attentive, never sleepy, never tired, never lagging, but always awake, alert, waiting for the visitation of the Christ, out of that silence, out of the infinity which is God, out of the depths of the Soul, comes either a voice, a feeling, a stirring, a release, or an assurance—call it any name you wish—and the error is dissolved and disappears.

It will make no difference whether the problem is physical, mental, moral, financial, or whether it is one of relationships, because it is not your wisdom that is undertaking the work.

You are not drawing now on what you have learned in your years of life on earth. You are holding yourself completely receptive to That which created you in the beginning and which knows the destiny of every person; and when you let It voice Itself, you will be back where you belong, which is under the jurisdiction of your heavenly Father, under the government of that *He* who knoweth your need before you do, He whose good pleasure it is to give you the kingdom.

Let the mind be an instrument of awareness and instead of trying to break your head against an apparently insoluble problem, worrying about what the next step should be or what you are to do tomorrow or the next day, form the habit of listening with your mind, using it as an instrument of awareness. Let God fill your mind. Be a witness to the Spirit motivating, animating, and permeating both the mind and body. Be a witness to It. Make of the mind and of the body instruments of God.

Through the mind become aware of the truth of God, and that truth will do the work, not your mind and not your thoughts. It is not the activity of your mind that frees anybody; it is *the activity of truth* in your mind that frees him.

You may have observed that in swimming, the more vigorously a person uses his body, the more quickly will he become exhausted, whereas the one who is completely relaxed in the water, resting on its surface, using his arms and feet to glide through the water rather than for the purpose of sustaining his body on top of the water, is able to remain afloat for a long, long time. The water holds the body up, the arms and legs merely propelling the body through the water, and the more relaxed a swimmer is, the longer will his body stay afloat.

The healing work is a beautiful work when it becomes as natural as floating on water or breathing. Otherwise, healing work can be harder, much harder than day labor. The spiritual healer anchored in spiritual wisdom remains relaxed in God and lets the Spirit flow. He lets the Truth flow, and then the

Truth sets him or his patient free. The Truth will do that; he never can.

That is the true sense of humility, a relaxing in the Spirit: " 'I can of mine own self do nothing'—even though I try. Just let me be relaxed and let the Truth carry the work." When you are swimming, let the water carry your body, and when you are giving a treatment, let the Spirit, let the Truth carry the treatment. Do not try to manipulate Truth with your mind. Truth is infinite, but the mind is finite; do not try to manipulate infinite Truth to fit into the pattern of the finite mind.

The mind is an instrument given to you for your use, just the same as is your body. We are not of those who deny the existence of a body or would throw the body out of the window, nor are we of those who would blank out or shut off the mind. The body is given to you so that you can move around in your present sphere of life. The body with its organs and functions, one integrated whole, is an instrument for your use: It is God's instrument to show forth His glory. Rightly speaking, the proper use of the body is to let God use the body, to let God govern and control the body. That leads to that relaxed state in which the government is on His shoulders. There is no way to aid digestion, assimilation, or elimination by taking thought. The mind was not given to you for that purpose. The mind is a vehicle through which you become aware of Truth, and that Truth will govern every organ and function of the body. Truth will strengthen your muscles; Truth will give you the capacity to know anything that you have need of knowing.

Every word of spiritual truth assimilated in your consciousness becomes a part of your mind and of your body. You do not control your body; you do not control your mind; but the activity of Truth in your consciousness, an activity which, of course, uses your mind, keeps your mind clear, active, clean, harmonious, and vital; and your mind, in its turn, manages, controls, and governs the body. The activity of Truth in your consciousness acts as a catalytic agent purifying both mind and body.

There is a spiritual Center in you, and in that Center is stored up your entire spiritual heritage—immortality, eternality, life, love, home, and infinite abundance. This Center is not within your body, and it is useless to look for it there. It is your consciousness, and that consciousness is not in your body: Your body is in your consciousness which is infinite. That is why, after you have studied and practiced, you will be able to close your eyes, be at peace, and find yourself in the body, out of the body, or wherever you would like to be; you will be able to draw out of the infinity of your own consciousness all that is necessary for your unfoldment from this day unto the end of the world and beyond it unto infinity.

Many people in metaphysics feel that the healing of physical ills through spiritual means is difficult because they do not understand the nature of the body. This misunderstanding stems from an incorrect concept of the word "matter." In fact, ever since the days of the first teaching of metaphysics, its followers have been confused by this term.

The majority of those using the term, "matter," usually in a quite glib fashion, have no understanding whatsoever of the true meaning of it. They have been taught that matter is unreal, that it is an illusion; they have been taught that matter has no life; and, inasmuch as matter constitutes the body, they have denied the reality and existence of the body in an attempt to overcome or get rid of it.

How can matter be unreal when it cannot be destroyed? Science has revealed that matter is an indestructible substance: Matter can change form, but it cannot be destroyed; it can be reduced to molecules and then to atoms; and when it has been resolved into atoms, what is left? Energy. Matter has not been destroyed by reducing it to its essence; matter has only changed form. There is no way to destroy matter because matter is indestructible. Actually, the substance of matter is mind: Matter is *mind appearing*, mind made visible as matter.

Water, for example, can change to steam or to ice, but in the process of change, it has not been destroyed. In fact, it weighs just as much in one form as in another. A glass tumbler can be reduced to splinters; it can be dissolved from human sight, but its component parts cannot be destroyed. In the laboratory, the technician can prove that it has existence and that that existence has weight.

"If matter is indestructible, how then," you may ask, "did this belief that matter is an illusion come about?"

The earliest recorded revelation as to the illusory nature of that which we see, hear, taste, touch, and smell is attributed to Gautama, the Buddha. On the basis of his revelation, he and his disciples did miracle-healing work. His later students, however, misunderstood the word "maya," or "illusion," and they interpreted illusion as something external to their being. When metaphysics was first given to the world in the last century, it was taught that our senses testify erroneously. Unfortunately, instead of holding to that, metaphysicians began to teach that everything existing in the external world is an illusion, including the body. *But this world is not an illusion*: It is the *concept* we entertain of it that is the illusion.

Spiritual healing is based on the premise that sin, disease, and death have no externalized reality: They exist only as illusory beliefs or concepts. But matter is not unreal; the body is not unreal; this world is not unreal: This world is beautiful, immortal, and eternal. This world will never be dissolved, but our concepts of it will change, just as our concepts of body change. Every adult will have to admit that he outgrew his concept of an infant body and put on a child's body; he outgrew that and took the body of a youth; and later he discarded his youthful body when he grew to the stature of maturity. Furthermore, as he progresses on the spiritual path, he will entertain a more spiritual *sense* of body, but never will he have a more spiritual body than he has now.

Probably more fun is poked at metaphysics and mysticism because of their use of the words "real," "unreal," "reality," and "unreality" than for any other reason. Metaphysicians are often ridiculed because some of them use such expressions as, "It is unreal," or "It is untrue." Two cars collide head-on and scatter themselves and those in them all over the scenery, and the metaphysician comes along and says, "Oh, it's unreal; it isn't true. It never happened." Can you blame the world for ridiculing such statements? The world does not understand the metaphysical meaning of the words "untrue" or "unreal," and the sad part is that very often the metaphysician using these same words does not understand the meaning of them either.

In the work of The Infinite Way, the words "real" or "reality" pertain only to that which is spiritual, eternal, immortal, and infinite. Only that which is of God is understood to be *real* or is recognized as *reality*. With this definition of reality in mind, it should be easy to grasp the statement that we cannot see, hear, taste, touch, or smell reality.

The words "unreal" and "unreality" pertain to anything, *whether to our sense harmonious or inharmonious*, that is not permanent.

It is at this point that the metaphysician usually makes his mistake. As a rule when he sees a healthy person or what he calls a good or moral person or a normal, healthy, harmonious situation, he is likely to think of that person or situation as real, but when he sees the sick or sinning, he calls that unreal. Such an interpretation is invalid in the light of the philosophic meaning of these words. Reality pertains only to that which is spiritual, is of Spirit, Soul, God, and therefore must be spiritually understood. It requires the faculty of the Soul to behold reality. Reality pertains only to that which is discerned through an inner awareness. Jesus referred to this as, "Having eyes, see ye not? and having ears, hear ye not?" In other words, there is that which must be seen and heard with the Soul-faculties.

When we speak of sin and disease as unreal, we do not mean that they are nonexistent. We are not just fooling ourselves and using our imagination in saying that they are unreal or untrue, but if a person has had ingrained in him from infancy that the material is the *real* and the material body the whole, then to him the disease is existent. When sin, disease, and death are called unreal, it is not a denial of the so-called existence of these things: It is a denial of their existence as a part of God or reality. Do you see the difference between these two statements?

In the realm of the real, the kingdom of God, the discords of sense have no existence. That, however, does not change the fact that we suffer from them. The unreality of it does not lessen our pain or remove our lack or limitation because, to our sense of things, we are suffering from them.

The beginning of wisdom is the realization that these conditions need not exist. Freedom from them comes not from seeking relief from God, but through seeking God and rising to that dimension of life in which only God is. There is not freedom *from* discord; there is not freedom *from* sin, false appetites, or desires; there is not freedom *from* poverty: There is only *freedom*—freedom in God, freedom in Spirit.

In filling yourself with the Spirit, you will find that spiritual law will operate in your experience in terms of all your needs. That is how the healing even of the body takes place, not because God thinks in terms of a sick physical body, nor even of a well physical body, but because, as you rise above the concepts of the physical into the realization of the Spirit, your consciousness is transformed and shows forth harmony in a language and a form you can understand.

Never, never use such statements as, "Oh, it is unreal," or "It is untrue," or "It never happened" unless you understand that what you are talking about is unreal and untrue and never happened *in the spiritual kingdom*. With that distinction in mind, you can accept the premise of the spiritual healing ministry that all sin, disease, lack, and limitation are unreal and that they are no part of reality.

The Master saw the unreality of power, evil power, when in response to Pilate's threat, "Knowest thou not that I have power to crucify thee, and have power to release thee?" he answered, "Thou couldest have no power at all against me, except it were given thee from above." Jesus recognized all the temporal power Pilate had, but he knew that in his own consciousness of reality, temporal power could not be exercised, nor could it operate. Again, when he was arrested, instead of resisting, he healed the soldier whose ear had been cut off by Peter; and later, on the cross, "Father, forgive them; for they know not what they do." He saw right through this human activity—saw it as unreal, that is, as not a part of the eternal, the immortal, and the forever lasting. It was this spiritual discernment which enabled him to come forth from the tomb. To his illumined spiritual consciousness, there was no power in the Crucifixion.

This same illumined spiritual consciousness—this Christ-consciousness—is here and now, and it is this consciousness which enables the spiritual healer of today to heal the sick and the sinning; it is the conviction that all forms of evil are unreal because they have no power to perpetuate themselves, no power to maintain or sustain themselves in the face of spiritual truth. Honor God in the realization that the spiritual kingdom is intact, and that whatever comes to your attention in the form of sin, disease, death, lack, or limitation is no part of reality, no part of the kingdom of God, and therefore has no witness, cannot stand, and has no substance or law to maintain it.

Let us assume that you have caught at least a glimpse of the underlying premise of spiritual healing which is that God appears *as*, and that sin, disease, and death are unreal because they are no part of God and have no existence in a consciousness elevated to spiritual awareness. Now let us go on to consider certain other terms frequently used in the healing ministry.

As a rule, disease is spoken of not as disease, but as a claim.

For example, consumption, cancer, or paralysis is referred to as a claim, a belief, or an appearance. You may ask as you read this, "Does changing the name do anything?" Yes, it does, because the healing work is an activity of consciousness, and unless these subtle phases of the healing ministry are clear to you there is no activity of truth in your consciousness to bring about healing.

Let me illustrate this. If you were traveling on the desert and saw, as is often the case, that the road ahead of you was covered with water, and if that were your first experience in the desert, you would automatically stop your car because obviously you could not drive through a sea of water. Your first thought would probably be, "What shall I do? How will I get through that water? How can the water be removed from the road?"

You look around and do not see any help. Then you look back again at the road, and if you look long enough, intently enough, you awaken to the fact that there is no water there. What you have been seeing is a mirage, an illusion. You smile, start your car, and go forward. As long as you were seeing water on the road, you would sit there helplessly waiting for that water to be removed, but the moment that you understood it to be a mirage, an illusion, the water disappeared, and you were free to go forward.

That is exactly the process in spiritual healing work. As long as you are dealing with a cancer, consumption, a tumor, paralysis, a cold, or influenza, you are at an impasse. What can you do about it? How can you get rid of it? What power have you to remove it? Or is there a God who can remove it? Too many prayers have been sent up to God to remove or change things or conditions so that we know that that does not work.

Then what *can* you do about it? As long as it remains a disease in your consciousness, you can do nothing about it. When, however, through illumined consciousness you come to see that it does not exist as disease, but that it exists only

as mirage, or illusion, then you have taken the first step in healing. Actually, healing is not difficult, regardless of the name or nature of the disease, if disease and sin become unreal in your consciousness. Strangely enough, one type of disease can become unreal in a person's consciousness, and he still might continue to have difficulty seeing the unreality of another form of disease.

One of my early experiences in spiritual healing illustrates this point. At that time, I was asked for help in a case of tuberculosis in which the patient, a young woman, was already being cared for in the "death shack," a place provided for those who were expected to pass within the next few days and where they were given good care, but were completely isolated from the other patients.

From the beginning, it required constant alertness: It took thirteen weeks of continuous work, hours and hours a day, before the doctors reported any significant improvement, and it was thirteen months before she left the sanatorium completely restored in health. To this day, she writes to me every Easter, Christmas, and Thanksgiving, always with the same story, that the only reason she ever goes to bed is to sleep. There is no sickness and has not been from that time to this.

The work that I did with her in that long period of time remained so indelibly impressed on me that every case of tuberculosis that has come to me in the years that have followed has been healed with the exception of one. The point I am trying to bring out through this experience is that healings take place, not through the intervention of some God, but through arriving at a state of consciousness in which sin, disease, and death have no reality, a consciousness which no longer battles these forms of discord and no longer tries to get rid of them. Our attitude toward them is the same as our attitude toward the water on the desert after we have discovered that it is not water, but an illusion, or mirage.

As long as disease is a reality to you, as long as you believe that fevers must run their course, or that they must be brought down, or that tumors must be reduced, or as long as you believe that the disease must follow some kind of a physical pattern, you are not in spiritual healing even though to some extent the Spirit may have been brought into the picture.

Complete total spiritual healing is the nonrecognition of the reality of the condition; it is a state of your consciousness or mine, or the practitioner's consciousness, in which God is so real and the works of God—the word of God, the universe of God, and the man of God—are so real that it is fantastic to believe that such a thing as disease of any kind could exist in God's universe.

The successful healing ministry is based, first of all, on the reality of God and the reality of God's creation whether appearing as man, body, or universe; and, in the second place, on the realization of the unreal nature of what is presenting itself to us as a sick or sinning person, as disease or as undesirable habits.

Let us understand the correct meaning of the terms "real" and "unreal"—their meaning in a spiritual sense. In other words, realize that whatever you behold through the physical senses is but a mirage which can be likened to the water on the desert. When you are able to do this, you will immediately translate illness into health. In fact, when you begin to discern spiritually, you will see something in everything around you—in flowers, clouds, stars, sunsets, sunrises—something greater than the human mind can grasp. Behind every externalized form, there is always more than the human mind or eye can comprehend. When you see with spiritual vision, you behold the man God made in His image and likeness, and it is this ability to discern reality which brings out healing.

CHAPTER V

WHAT DID HINDER YOU?

A s children you have all played the game where you make chalk marks, little squares, on the sidewalk. Somebody chases you until you are inside one of the square boxes and you cannot get out until you pay a forfeit. Who says you cannot get out? There is only a chalk mark there to keep you in, but the rules of the game say you must remain there, and so you do.

That is good fun as long as it is a game, but would it not be tragic if the other children went home while you were in that box and did not release you, and you felt that you could not get out of the box? And yet, all you would have had to do would have been to step across those lines.

The Master, Christ Jesus, watched people imprisoned by "chalk marks"—multitudes of them. They sat crippled at the gates and in the streets, but he merely looked at them and said, "Wilt thou be made whole? . . . Rise, take up thy bed, and walk." And they arose and walked. They found that there was nothing hindering them: They were just obeying a rule of human life which says that under certain conditions or at a certain age a person may be paralyzed, and this they had accepted. Jesus saw the chalk mark there, and in his conviction that there was nothing hindering them, they got up and walked. To Lazarus, he said, "Lazarus, come forth," and Lazarus came forth. What was hindering him? The rules of the game of human life! So people will continue to suffer until somebody comes along who sees that the laws of sin, disease, and lack are chalk marks and, in his spiritual discernment, asks, "What did hinder you?"

The Master told us that we must become as little children in order to accept the truth. Very often the reason for delayed healings is the spiritual healer's inability to be childlike enough to see a white chalk line where somebody else has seen a death date or has accepted a certain period as necessary for the disease to run its course.

People see three chalk marks instead of one when it is an incurable disease, and they are locked more tightly than ever in their prison. An incurable disease! What can be worse than that? As a matter of actual fact, spiritual healing often has far greater success with incurable diseases than with the curable ones because when a doctor says, "I've done all I can do," the patient gives up hope of a cure from *materia medica* and, in his hopelessness, he is receptive and responsive to the spiritual impulse.

Only those white chalk marks, called time, diagnoses, symptoms, or appearances, can make you believe that you are a prisoner of disease or sin. The only requirement for freedom is to skip across that line. And why not? What is hindering you? A belief? A theory? When you recognize it as but a belief or theory, all the white chalk lines begin to disappear out of your life because they are not there as barriers: They are there only as appearances.

When Peter was in prison, all the iron bars and locks were real and seemingly impossible to break. Then the angel of the Lord appeared, the miracle happened, and he was outside the prison—but the bars were still there, and the locks were still there.

Hezekiah told his people in their moment of battle when they were facing a superior enemy, "With him is an arm of flesh; but with us is the Lord our God to help us, and to fight our battles." When you are faced with a problem—physical, mental, moral, or financial—remember, "This is but the arm of flesh, trying to convince me that it is a power, but it has no power. It is only an arm of flesh."

Bunch together all the errors—sin, disease, infection, contagion, death, lack, limitation, weather, climate—and summarily dispose of them as the "arm of flesh," not worth fighting. Then you will begin to heal and not until then. You bring yourself close to the kingdom of God when God becomes the all-in-all and when every problem is dismissed as the "arm of flesh," the white chalk line—no hindrance, nothingness—because you have come to understand the true nature of God as Infinity, Omnipresence, Omniscience, infinite Wisdom, divine Love.

Intellectually knowing this is inspiring; entertaining it in thought is a grand experience; but one day something comes right up in front of you and says: "I am a beggar; I am a cripple; I am a cold; I am a cancer, consumption, unemployment, lack and limitation!" and you begin to tremble all over. Then you discover that whereas you have been voicing the Word, you have not yet come face to face with the reality of it, and now you must begin to put it into practice and face this so-called enemy.

Face it; look right at it; and see if you cannot translate it into a white chalk mark, or the "arm of flesh," and thereby come to that absolute conviction, "*I*,[1] God, in the midst of me is the all-in-all. You out there—you are just a white chalk mark, the 'arm of flesh.'"

Just for a moment imagine that you are experiencing an unpleasant night dream: You are in the ocean, swimming; you have gone out too far; you look back toward the shore and see that there is very little hope of rescue. Even though you shout your lungs out, no one can hear you. And so you are seized with fear. You struggle and strive to reach the shore, and, of course, the harder you fight, the harder the ocean fights you. There is only one thing left for you to do—drown. Yes, drown—but wait! In your fight, you shouted and some-

[1] Wherever "I" appears in italics, the reference is to God.

one heard you, came over and shook you, woke you up, and behold the miracle! The drowning self disappeared; the ocean disappeared; the struggle disappeared. You awakened and found that you had never left your comfortable home. All that was necessary in order to be released from the struggle was *to awaken*.

This is the nature of spiritual healing. Whether you are struggling with some form of sin, false appetite, disease, poverty, unemployment, or unhappiness, stop struggling and wake up. Wake up to your true identity. You are not a swimmer in a deep ocean; you are not a sufferer in sin and disease: You are the Christ-consciousness, a child of God, and the very error you are fighting, you are perpetuating by that fighting.

There is no need to struggle. Relax in the realization that in all this universe, there is only God appearing as you and me: God's own undivided Selfhood is individualized as you and me. Divine harmony is your destiny. It is the destiny of every individual whether he is living in good health or bad, whether he is living in saintliness or sinfulness. The ultimate destiny of every one of us is divine harmony—*when we awaken*. "I shall be satisfied, when I awake, with thy likeness."

When you begin to grasp the meaning of awakening, then you will realize that the so-called errors of this world, the sins and diseases, lacks and limitations, do not exist as actual conditions or states of being, but as illusory pictures or concepts in mind. That makes them just as painful or annoying as they were when you were suffering from them, but it also makes it possible for you to be healed of them. You cannot be healed spiritually while you accept a sin, a disease, or a lack as an actual condition. It is only possible to heal spiritually when you know the unreal nature of that which is causing the trouble in your experience.

Those of you who have studied metaphysics have been taught that the nature of sin and disease is illusion; you have been taught to call it mortal mind, or nothingness. With most students, that illusion or that mortal mind or nothingness still remains as something to be healed or removed, but nobody should have anything to get rid of after he knows that what has been troubling him is an illusion. If somebody saw a ghost over in the corner and said, "Get rid of it," you would understand that he was seeing the ghost as an "it" in the corner, but after he had awakened to the fact that it was an illusion, what would you think of him if he persisted in saying, "Get rid of it"?

Once you perceive that that which Jesus called "this world," that is, the material sense of a universe, is really an illusion, you will know why the great Master could overcome the world. He overcame it through the understanding that it was an illusion: Therein lay the overcoming, and if you are to follow the example set by Jesus, you, too, will have to learn that the only way in which you can overcome "this world" is through knowing that a thing is not the thing you perceive it to be; a condition is not the condition you perceive it to be; a person is not the person you perceive him to be. What you are dealing with always is illusion, and knowing that it is an illusion should dissolve it, and will, if there is real conviction in your knowing.

All the discord in the world is the product of the mind when it is distorted by ignorance. This state of incomplete apprehension of the real and eternal is often spoken of in The Infinite Way as a state of hypnotism. Anyone who has watched the response of a nation or of a crowd to propaganda should be able readily to understand how easily mass hypnotism can be produced when those affected are under stress and strain. In such cases, there is no person acting as a hypnotist *per se*, nor is there a specific subject upon whom he works, but nevertheless the effect produced is hypnotic in that it is "characterized by marked susceptibility to suggestion and loss of will power."[2] Those affected by it had nothing to do with its promulgation or dissemination and are a part of

[2] *American College Dictionary* (New York: Random House, 1958).

it only as victims of mass hypnotism.

An individual is, in a sense, born hypnotized by the very fact of being born into the human predicament. Everyone about him perceives the material manifestation as the real existence so that he, too, falls under the spell. In other words, he is hypnotized. There is a universal mesmerism which strikes one person as disease, one as false appetite, one as sensuality, one as poverty, and another as something else. It is a universal hypnotism, and everybody by virtue of having been conceived in his mother's womb is a victim of it.

The effect of this universal hypnotism is to make a person accept disease, death, lack, limitation, unemployment, depression, wars, or accidents as reality. Lay the ax at the root of the tree: Do not bother about picking off the branches; do not bother about healing a little piece of flesh here and a little false appetite there. Realize that in healing you are not dealing with a person or a condition *per se*: You are dealing with universal hypnotism.

To help you arrive at an understanding of the universal nature of hypnotism, I call to your mind the studies in subliminal perception that have been made in recent years. It has been found that many people respond to suggestions of which they are not even aware. For example, in a motion picture theater where these experiments were being conducted, slides, instructing the audience to go into the lobby during the intermission to buy popcorn and Coca Cola, were flashed upon the screen so rapidly as to be imperceptible. Even though these slides were invisible to the eye and did not register consciously in the mind, people in the audience went downstairs in unprecedented numbers and bought Coca Cola and popcorn which they may not particularly have wanted. They did not hear anybody tell them to do it; they did not consciously see any advertising; but they responded to suggestions which they did not even know they had received and, thereby, found themselves acting out something of which they themselves had no knowledge. It is plain that if these suggestions had been made directly to them with their knowledge, they could have used their judgment or discrimination as to whether or not they should buy.[3]

If you understand how this mesmerism operates, you will know why it is that everybody is a victim of the ills of this world until he comprehends the nature of these errors. Those people in the theater could just as well have picked up, "You have a cold." They could just as well have picked up, "You have cancer," or "You have fear." You know this is true because you have undoubtedly had many days when you have felt fearful without knowing whence or why it came. But had you gone outside, you probably would have seen a headline in a newspaper; or had you turned on your radio, you might have found that the radio headlines were blaring forth some story of disaster. Your fear was the result of a universal hypnotism. It was not you; it was that universal thing that runs from person to person, place to place, situation to situation, and all of a sudden you find yourself a victim of it.

Such an approach is quite different from that used in most mental healing, whether it is accomplished through one of the modern mental science organizations or whether it is accomplished by psychology or psychiatry, all of which rest primarily upon the thesis that lurking in a person's thought is error of some kind, and if only it can be rooted out, healing will follow. Cancer, tuberculosis, arthritis—whatever the disease—all are attributed to erroneous thinking or to some undesirable trait of character on the part of the patient. Some practitioners probe into the human mind in an attempt to "uncover the error," to point out to the patient that his problems stem from his jealousy, sensuality, miserliness, malice, or hatred. It would seem that some problems apparently do stem from these undesirable qualities. On the human level of life and as long as a human being lives in

[3] For a further discussion of this subject see the author's *The 1958 Infinite Way Letters* (London: L. N. Fowler & Co., Ltd., 1959), pp. 200-218.

the world, he is inevitably such a part of the world consciousness that he unsuspectingly and unknowingly takes on the
complexion of that consciousness.

Perhaps you have had the experience of being told that if
you had been just a little more loving or a little more generous or a little more grateful or a little sweeter to some relative, you would not now be struggling with whatever your
particular problem may be, and that if you hope to have
a healing you will have to begin to be forgiving, kind, loving,
considerate, patient, or generous. That is psychology; that is
mind science in which your physical or mental disease is
usually laid at the door of a mental cause.

Furthermore, mental treatment is directed at the patient.
Sometimes the name of the patient is taken into the treatment or the name of the disease: "Jane Smith, you are God's
perfect child. You are well and you know it. You are spiritual.
Jane Smith, you are free; Jane Smith, you are perfect; Jane
Smith, you are this; Jane Smith, you are that." That is the
way the treatment is addressed, although the truth is that
Jane Smith, a human being, is not any of these things. All
that such a metaphysician knows about God and the image
and likeness of God is being pounded into Jane as if Jane
were already that. By hammering away at Jane, telling her
that she is already spiritual and perfect, the mental scientist
hopes to make her become that.

Spiritual healing is entirely different from any of these
approaches. In spiritual healing, as taught and practiced in
The Infinite Way, there is no mental cause, that is, no
individual mental cause for physical disease. True, there is a
mental cause for a physical effect, but it is not personal to
the individual: It is a universal mesmerism in human consciousness, a universal belief in a selfhood apart from God,
which is hypnotic in its effect.

Under this universal hypnosis, no matter what the disease,
the patient is no more responsible for it than he is responsible for the wrong thinking that is supposed to have produced

it. Do not be so "metaphysical" as to believe that he brought it on himself with his wrong thinking—or maybe grandma did. Do not believe it! He is no more responsible for that wrong thinking than he is for the so-called effects of the wrong thinking because in both cases he is but a victim of a universal belief, a universal hypnotism, which he has accepted and which you and I have accepted.

In other words, if you are jealous, envious, or dishonest, you are not to be condemned for it, and furthermore, you are never going to be free from these errors until someone or some understanding comes into your experience to show you how to correct them. You will not correct them merely by trying to be a better human being; you will not be able to correct them by deciding, "I am going to stop being jealous," or "I am going to stop being dishonest." It cannot be done that way; it has been tried for generations and has not succeeded, and it will not succeed now.

Something more is needed. Something must be introduced into your consciousness which will free you from wrong thinking and which will make wrong thinking an impossibility in your experience. The first step is to stop condemning yourself: Stop blaming yourself for your sins; stop blaming yourself for your shortcomings; stop blaming yourself for your errors. You will get nowhere by condemning either yourself or your neighbor. Remove this condemnation from yourself and realize that to whatever degree you are expressing negative qualities of mind and body, to that extent you have permitted world beliefs to be imposed upon you.

Begin to understand that the nature of your being is God, the nature of your Soul is God, the nature of your mind is God, and the nature of your body is the temple of God. Your very body is the temple of the living God: Stop condemning it; stop hating it; stop fearing it. Your mind is an instrument through which God, Truth, can flow: Do not condemn your mind and do not call it a bad mind or a mortal mind or a material mind. There are no such minds; there is only one mind and that mind is an instrument of God. When you stop condemning your mind, you will find that your mind is a clear transparency for the Soul.

If you have had any experience at all with pets or with children, you must certainly know that condemning and punishing them and telling them how bad they are, or how naughty or wicked, is no way to bring out the good in them. That is no way to bring out the good in anyone or anything. The way to bring out good in a child or an animal, or a flower or any growing thing is to love it, to bless it, to realize that God is the very essence of its being and that God constitutes its nature.

When a person comes to you for help, do not sit in judgment on him; do not criticize him; do not blame him; do not look around for his sins of omission or commission because even if he has any they are only effects. They are not cause. Behind every fault and failure, there is a cause, but the cause is never personal: The cause is a universal hypnotism.

This explains how people become sick or sinful, how they develop false appetites and desires, why they are weak enough to get drunk or foolish enough to be reckless in their driving. It is not that they themselves want to be that way: This universal hypnotism strikes people unbeknownst to themselves, acting upon them so that when the world says it is raining outside, thousands of people catch cold.

A spiritual healer is a person who understands that he is not dealing with colds, with cancer, consumption, or polio. He is not dealing with prenatal influences; he is not dealing with change of life or old age: He is dealing with a misapprehension of reality—hypnotism, mesmerism, suggestion. These are not entities or identities. Hypnotism is something that causes a mental image, but that mental image is always without substance, law, or cause, and the moment the hypnotism is destroyed, the image is also destroyed.

Let us see how this process operates. Close your eyes: Turn

your mind to a street, any street you like, any street you know. Look at the houses there—all kinds and descriptions, here a brick one, there a stone one, and over there a wooden one. Out in front of these are fresh green lawns, and over in this lawn a rose bed and over on that one asters or zinnias. There are scores of children playing, and in the street an occasional automobile rushes by. You might even picture one of the children running out in front of one of the speeding vehicles and hear the screeching of the brakes and a child's scream.

The doorbell rings, or the telephone. Immediately you open your eyes. The dream is gone. Where are all the houses, the children, and the accident? They have vanished, because a dream cannot create houses, a dream cannot create children, a dream cannot create accidents. A dream-substance can create nothing but substanceless images. So it is with hypnotism. A hypnotist can make you see a dozen donkeys dancing in your room, but there will not be one there. On the other hand, suppose you are so hypnotized that you are certain the donkeys are there. How are you going to get rid of them? There is only one way—break the hypnotism. Break the hypnotism by calling upon the subject to awaken, and then what happens to the forms? They disappear.

In spiritual healing, whether the claim is named Jones, Brown, or Smith; whether the claim is named cancer, consumption, or polio; whether the claim is called unemployment, depression, or unhappy relationships; do not be tricked into treating persons or conditions. Leave them alone and get back to the substanceless substance to which you can give any name you like—the carnal mind, hypnotism, suggestion. It can be anything *as long as you interpret it as meaning nothingness*—no substance, no law, no cause.

When you really begin to comprehend that in healing you are not dealing with people as people, when you learn to eliminate them and their specific claims from your thought, and in every instance deal with the root of the problem—the carnal mind, nothingness; the "arm of flesh," nothingness—

you will find how quickly you will be able to become consciously aware of a spiritual Presence within you. This Presence cannot be felt until you are free of the barrier: The barrier is the belief in two powers; the barrier is the belief in something apart from God.

If you prefer, the word, "temptation," can be used in place of hypnotism. When you feel ill, you might look upon that as a temptation coming to you for acceptance or rejection. The only way you can reject the temptation is to recognize it as the "arm of flesh," or nothingness, no matter what is brought to you, whatever its name or nature, no matter who it is.

The carnal mind is not the opposite of a divine mind, and you are not looking for a divine mind to do something to a carnal mind. The minute you have made the carnal mind a nothingness, the "arm of flesh," you no longer have two powers and you can do just what it says in Scripture, rest in His word. You can rest in this Word, waiting for the Spirit of the Lord God to be upon you; and when it comes, it breaks the hypnotism.

For years after I had learned to recognize that all forms of sin, disease, lack, limitation, depression, or whatnot are mesmeric sense, or hypnotism, the puzzle was to discover how to break that hypnotism for a person. What could I do? A hypnotist just snaps his fingers, and his subject awakens, or he wills him to awaken. This I could not do because, on the spiritual path, I am not permitted to use physical or mental power.

It was then that I discovered that scriptural passage which you will find throughout all my writings, "the stone was cut out of the mountain without hands." By the time I had spent some months puzzling on its obscure meaning, the answer began to be apparent: The weapon against error—our offense and defense—is something that is neither physical nor mental, no action, no words, no thoughts—only the awareness of God.

As you carry this out in practice, watching the stone being formed in and of your consciousness while you stand to one side as a witness or a beholder, eventually a state of peace will come. Then you will catch a glimpse of God as *Is*—not a power over anything, just *God is*. You begin to understand that no power does anything to anyone, and you become a beholder as reality begins to appear. All problems fade out in proportion as you develop this ability to be quiet, to behold, and to witness divine harmony unfold, and because of the principle of oneness, your patient experiences this harmony.

The principle behind this process is that, inasmuch as the activity of the human mind is the substance and the activity of hypnotism, when the human mind is not functioning, there is no more hypnotism. When you are not thinking thoughts or words, when you are in a stillness, the human mind is stopped—the hypnotism is gone. When you experience this, you will feel something which transcends the human dimension of life.

Do not battle the forms of error: Do not try to lop off rheumatism or consumption or cancer. Do not try to lop off old age. Do not try to change the appearance-world. Get back, get back! Realize that in reality God constitutes your being, and the only thing from which you are suffering is a universal belief in two powers. Get back and rest in the Word. If you battle one phase of error and defeat it, ten others may pop up to take its place. You have to wipe out that which is the cause of the human discord. And what is that? The fabric of nothingness, this so-called carnal mind which is not a power except to those who are eternally fighting evil.

If, with every claim that comes to you, you can set aside any thought of the person involved, his name and the nature of the claim, and can go back to some word or term which to you represents nothingness—not something that has to be fought against, not something that has to be risen

above, but just nothingness, so that you have only one power
—then you can sit in meditation and you will feel the descent
of the Holy Ghost; you will feel the peace that passes understanding; you will feel a divine Presence and a release from
fear or discord.

Consciously remember as you go into your meditation
that you are not praying for the purpose of changing, healing, reforming, or correcting anything or anybody. Establish
this clearly in your mind: "I am going into meditation, but
there is no person involved and no condition involved. My
meditation has nothing to do with a person, and it has
nothing to do with a condition. It has to do with realizing
a spiritual Presence right where I am. So now I am going
to be silent and let that realization take place."

All that is necessary for harmony is God's grace realized.
You do not have to know a lot of deep metaphysics: You
have to know the simple things, the very simple things, such
as the revelation of one power and the nothingness of the
"armies of the aliens." You understand that God is something more than a word. God is much more even than a long
list of synonyms: God is an experience, and no one knows
God until he has had that experience.

PART TWO

SPIRITUAL HEALING:

THE ROLE OF TREATMENT

CHAPTER VI

DEVELOPING A HEALING CONSCIOUSNESS

Treatment is a technique employed to lift consciousness to such an elevation that a contact with God is established which permits spiritual power to flow into human activity. It is a recognition of spiritual truth, the purpose of which is to reveal an already existing state of divine harmony. This realization on the part of the person giving the treatment reveals the spiritual identity of the one who has asked for healing so that he can be seen as he spiritually is in God's image and likeness.

As has been pointed out, anyone who practices spiritual healing must rise above the level of appearances—above the discords of corporeal sense, of personal sense—to a higher plane of consciousness where there is no person to be healed and where there is room only for the Spirit of God.

Treatment is necessary only because a belief of humanhood has become ingrained in individual consciousness. This humanhood, or personal sense, cannot be overcome by trying to be good or by trying to think good thoughts, because any such attempt would merely be a shift from bad humanhood to good humanhood. Such a shift is, of course, desirable humanly, and naturally nearly everybody in the human picture comes eventually to see that human good is better than human evil and desires to be good rather than evil. That, however, is not spiritual demonstration, but only a step forward in human evolution.

Real spiritual progress begins when a person is no longer preoccupied with either human good or evil, health or disease, wealth or poverty, but is able to penetrate beyond these to the Christhood which is his spiritual identity. Through such spiritual vision, that which has heretofore been identified as error, or evil, normally and naturally disappears because it is no part of spiritual consciousness. Jesus demonstrated this spiritual consciousness again and again. Although he spoke to his followers in terms of their experience— "Martha, thou art . . . troubled . . ."—he demonstrated spiritual consciousness which sees beyond the apparent to the real. After all, he was the Christ, one with the Father. When we achieve this Christ-consciousness, then we too achieve the single-eyed vision.

That may be hard to grasp, especially when we are engulfed by the vicissitudes of life. But consider for a moment the reason human beings are beset by so many problems. For generations, we have been prodigals, living on our own substance out in the world, not drawing on the Father, but living off one another to such a degree that we have lost the awareness of our true identity. Within us, this Christ, this child or emanation of God, lies dormant, covered over with layers and layers of human beliefs built up throughout the centuries. Human beings have been away from the Father's house so long that they have forgotten that their parentage is of God.

In this age, man's true Self is again being revealed, and the time has come when he must awaken to the nature and character of his being, to that Christhood which is his spiritual destiny. In this awakening process, he dies to his humanhood that he may be reborn of the Spirit.

A treatment is a rising in consciousness above that which can be seen, heard, tasted, touched, or smelled in order to perceive that which is real. Just as the motorist on a desert highway does not look around to find buckets with which to remove the water from the road, but recognizes that he is only facing a mirage and in that knowledge proceeds on his way; so to the Christ-consciousness there are no impediments. When that state of Christ-consciousness is attained, a person can look at the water on the road, the tracks coming together, the sky sitting on the mountain, and still know in his heart:

These states of limitation do not exist. They are merely images of the mind—appearances—but the truth is that the kingdom of God, the realm of eternal life and harmony, is within me. It is not to be achieved; it is already within me. Because of this, I can always turn within and come into the full realization of the Kingdom, now. My only function is to become aware of its is-ness, to realize that it already is, and therefore I have nothing to seek.

Knowing the truth, declaring and thinking about the truth are mental processes; they are steps that lead to spiritual discernment. But such mental processes do not heal anything, nor do they bring harmony into individual experience. The purpose of treatment is to lift consciousness to that point where spiritual discernment or realization takes place.

There is a procedure in treatment which may prove helpful. First of all, when a person asks for help, assure him that he will be given help; then drop the name or identity of the person and recognize the nature of the claim as of the carnal mind. Do not think of the patient, the body, or the condition again; but turn immediately to *God.* Keep your mind stayed on God. Your meditation may take some such form as this:

What do I know about God? "In the beginning God." God made all that was made, and all that God made was good. Anything that God did not make was not made. Therefore, since we have a body, God made that body, and it must be made of the substance of God—perfect, spiritual, harmonious. In the body of God's creating, there cannot be

*a cause for disease or pain, nor can there be an effect such
as disease, pain, discord, or inharmony.*

*God is life eternal. If God is life eternal, there certainly
cannot be a presence or a power anywhere in heaven or on
earth to lessen that eternality, to change it, to alter it, or to
interfere with it. Therefore, in the allness of God, no cause
for pain can be found, no cause of disease, and no effect such
as pain or disease. God is the substance of all being, for God
is the substance of which the universe is made.*

*God is law, the only law. If God is the only law, there
cannot be a law of inharmony, such as a law of disease, a law
of separation, infection, or contagion. They are not reality,
and they are not cause. God alone is the law, and God is
the law of harmony unto His creation, maintaining and sustaining it.*

*God is love, and since God is infinite, Love is the all-power
and the all-presence. Love is that which cares for Its own.*

If God, divine Love, is caring for Its own, must it not be
clear that the law and the love of God are sufficient to maintain God's creation harmoniously, joyously, and perfectly?

Notice that the treatment is always a recognition of the
nothingness of the condition and deals only with God and
the qualities of God—God as infinite Good, the infinite All,
the infinite Presence, the infinite Effect. Finally, the realization is achieved that God really is all-in-all, and besides
God there is nothing else, and by that time, you will have
come to see that there cannot be such a thing as a patient
because there could not be a person, personality, or individu-
ality apart from God, nor could there be a condition or
circumstance apart from God.

Know every bit of truth you can know; take every syno-
nym for God you can possibly find and see it in its relationship to individual being. Every truth you know about God
is the truth about individual man, since the principle is that
God and man are one.

To know the truth about God, but to think of that truth as something separate and apart from man, or to think of man as being sick or sinning and in need of God is to lose the effect of the treatment. The treatment must embody the realization of the great truth that "he that seeth me seeth him that sent me," whether that "he" is Bill Jones, Mary Jane, or anybody else. God and His manifestation are one; God and His individualization are one.

There are thousands of forms of treatment. One morning in answer to a call, God gave me the strangest treatment that has ever come to me in all my years of work. The words I heard were, "God, the Father; God, the Son; God, the Holy Ghost." That was all. I did not understand it. So I sat there with, "God, the Father; God, the Son; God, the Holy Ghost." I must have repeated those words a dozen times very slowly, trying to see if I could get a meaning out of it, and then like a burst of light it came: "Why yes, you know that God is the Father. Certainly, God is the Father, but God is also the Son. Are we not all sons of the one Father? Well, then, no son of God can be in any trouble or difficulty as long as he realizes his sonship. And the Holy Ghost? That is our awareness or understanding of this oneness of God and man." The treatment was as simple as that, and the healing took place with the realization that God is the only being, the only identity, eternally about the Father's business of glorifying the Father.

A treatment can last all day or all night, or it can be of a minute's duration. Whatever its length, it is a good treatment if it leads back to the realization of God as individual being. Every treatment should be spontaneous because a ready-made treatment is of less value than no treatment at all. Certainly no two treatments should or will be alike. Therefore, do not try to use the same treatment tomorrow that you used today. You might give the most powerful treatment in the world today, one which lifts you to a place in consciousness where somebody is raised from the dead, and yet find that tomorrow it might not even heal a headache. If you are called upon to give a hundred treatments in a day, they must be a hundred different treatments.

The use of words—formulas or statements of truth in the sense of treatment—is as useless as trying to get today's news out of yesterday's newspaper or trying to pick yesterday's manna. Manna falls fresh every day, and in the same way, inspiration flows fresh with every demand made upon it; therefore, do not try to use the inspiration of today for a treatment tomorrow. Inspiration will come at any moment that there is a need, because your heavenly Father knoweth that you have need of these things.

There is no one treatment or form of treatment that meets every need. This is because all human beings live at different levels. Furthermore, not only is each person at a different state or stage of consciousness, but any one person is at a different stage of consciousness on different days. Inasmuch as no one is always on the same level of consciousness, a treatment must meet the needs of the particular state of consciousness of the particular person on the particular day.

Every call for help always involves a person or persons— a condition of the body, a condition of business, or a condition of the mind. Nevertheless, whatever the nature of the problem, the treatment is a realization of the problem as but the carnal mind, and the treatment always remains on the level of God.

If, for example, a call for help should come in connection with marital difficulties, you would remember that, as a practitioner, you have no advice to offer, and, therefore, you have nothing to do with the human aspects of the case because the human picture has no relationship whatsoever to the divine. Never come down to the level of trying to patch up quarrels; never come down to the level of trying to hold couples together or of trying to bring about a separation.

Spiritual work is not a patching up of the human scene: It is an understanding that what is appearing to us as a problem is a suggestion of a selfhood apart from God, hav-

St. Charles City-County Library District

Spencer Road (SP)

427 Spencer Road
St. Peters, MO 63376
(636) 447-2320
10/21/2013 4:26:45 PM

cess "Your Account" to renew your materials at:
ww.youranswerplace.org

nes charged on late items.
renewal on reserved items.

rary Card: 9006589535

All Items Out (1)

ys in the lives of social workers : 54
ol./Ed. 3rd.ed 2005
all #: 361 32097 Days
C #: 1019160683   Due: 11/04/2013

* * * Opt in and go green! * * *

gin to 'your account' to sign up:
overdue notices by email
due date reminders by email
library newsletters by email

youraccount.youranswerplace.org

ing no more substance than the water on the desert. With this awareness then comes the realization of God as the only Being, complete and whole. That realization would bring an assurance and with it would come a sense of peace. If the assurance did not come, then I would sit down again and establish the peace and quiet within myself until the feeling came that all was well.

Another call may come from a person who is ill. When a claim involves something dealing with activity, such as the activity of the heart or the lungs, instantly would come the recognition that this is a mental image, and I would realize God as omni-action, God as the only activity of life, of being, and of body; and thereby establish that sense of God-action and God-being.

You must have noticed by now that the entire treatment is a recognition of the nonpower of the condition; it deals only with God and is always on the level of God, not on the level of mortal man. Furthermore, the treatment is given almost before the telephone receiver is put back on the hook; or, if the request for help has come by way of a letter, it is accomplished before I have reached the bottom of the page. However, if I did not immediately sense that all was well, I would sit back for a moment, meditate, find my inner peace, realize my oneness with God—and this is treatment.

If, an hour or two later, a case should come back to my thought with a feeling of urgency, I would give another treatment because the very fact that it has come back to my mind indicates that it is undoubtedly unfinished business. Again, the realization is that this problem is but an appearance and that God is the only life—indivisible, inseparable, and perfect.

At the moment of realization, your treatment is complete. This may be the very moment when your patient is healed. However, the healing is not always immediately apparent. There are many reasons for a delayed response. One thing, though, to be borne in mind is that the healing of a specific dis-ease—physical, mental, or whatever—is not the aim of spiritual healing.

The demonstration is the realization of God. Therefore, if you begin any treatment by asking, "Father, what is the nature of this demonstration?" very quickly the answer may come in some such form as this:

Demonstrate Me. Demonstrate that I am a living, moving being in your life. Demonstrate that I am present in you. Demonstrate that I am as vital in you as I was in my Son, Jesus Christ.

Unless you go to God for but one purpose—for God and God alone—you are acknowledging two powers, good and evil, and you are expecting God, the big good Power, to do something to the nasty little evil power. Rest will never come, nor will peace, as long as you are waiting for a great big God to do something to an error. Peace will come only when you can sit quietly in the realization:

Thank You, Father, all I expect of Your word is that it will burst the bubble, pierce the veil, because harmony already is. I would not be here waiting to hear Your voice if I believed there were inharmony and discord.

You should want God only for the purpose of God-realization. What God does to you or to your affairs is an entirely different matter. The minute you try to direct God to bring you companionship or a home, an occupation or a talent, God then becomes the means to an end. That is shocking when you stop to think about it; it is almost blasphemous— this idea of using God—and yet the commonly accepted concept of prayer and treatment is that God will do something for you, or that by your words God can be influenced in the right direction. That is not prayer, and that is why most prayer is not effective. The only effective prayer is the attainment of God-realization.

Usually the second half of the treatment is much shorter

than the first half, and even though it is the more important part, it is one which many metaphysicians disregard entirely. They think that the treatment they have given is the healing agency, and that is the reason so many treatments are not successful.

Once again, I must repeat, *you* do not give the treatment that heals: You are but the vehicle through which it comes. Your treatment is merely to prepare your consciousness for the receptivity of the *real* treatment, the word of God which comes to you from God within. Into the state of receptivity which has been developed through knowing the truth, the word of God pours itself forth: God gives the treatment which does the actual healing work.

The ultimate of treatment is reached when no words, no statements of truth, no affirmations, and no denials are used. That is the ultimate state, but not only cannot everyone attain that state, but no one I have ever known has been able to maintain it continuously. Therefore, from time to time, there is a reverting to a form of treatment that has in it some words and some thoughts. However, it must be understood that no treatment is complete until some measure of inner assurance has been achieved. It does not make too much difference what form of treatment you use to raise yourself up to that point where you receive that inner release which assures you that the treatment is complete, but it does make a difference that you do not consider the treatment complete until you have had this feeling of peace within yourself.

Treatment clears your thought of superstitions, ignorance, and false theories and makes of it a transparency for *"My thoughts."* You will never be a healer: You may be a practitioner, but you will never be a healer. The sense of peace that comes to you—the peace that passes understanding— is the healer. When you attain that, healing takes place. It is the awareness of God that does the healing.

CHAPTER VII

PRACTICAL INSTRUCTIONS TO WORKERS

The first requisite for any person who practices spiritual healing, even if only for himself, is a developed spiritual consciousness because all healing is the result of individual consciousness, yours or mine. It is not dependent on God; it is not dependent on God-consciousness or Christ-consciousness in the abstract, *but upon individual consciousness lifted to the heights of Christ-consciousness,* which is the God-power that makes it possible to do the works of God. If, however, the practitioner does not keep his consciousness filled with truth and love, those who touch him on life's highway will not find him doing the works of God, spreading harmony and peace abroad in the world.

Jesus, the greatest spiritual healer ever known, lived, moved, and had his being continuously in the realization of the Father within, and for that reason he could do the works of God and state with conviction: "He that seeth me seeth him that sent me." Undoubtedly if at this moment you had a problem and were given the opportunity of choosing a practitioner out of all the world and out of all time, you would immediately turn to Jesus Christ in the complete assurance of receiving your healing. But, if it is God who heals or if it is impersonal, abstract God-consciousness or Christ-consciousness, why would you particularly want Jesus Christ? Is it not because Jesus Christ, insofar as our knowledge goes, had the greatest degree of unfolded and realized God-consciousness?

If it were not possible for you to have the aid of Jesus, to whom would you turn then? From your knowledge of Scripture, it would probably be to John, and then to Peter or Paul because they demonstrated in their healing work the tremendous depth of their spiritual capacity and spiritual awareness.

Always the healer is the consciousness of any individual who has attained some measure of Christ-consciousness, and the measure attained determines the degree of the healing work. There are those who believe that the ability to heal is some special gift conferred upon a few chosen people and which therefore becomes their exclusive prerogative. But actually a practitioner is a degree of developed consciousness of truth, and, in the degree that he is imbued with truth, will his consciousness have power.

By the grace of God, God's consciousness is realized as individual consciousness. "But how," you may ask, "how do I attain this consciousness? How do I achieve it? How do I bridge the gap from being a businessman or a housewife to becoming an instrument for spiritual healing?"

At every step of your unfoldment, it is well to remember that no spiritual progress can be made without the grace of God, and that, of yourself, you cannot succeed regardless of how determined you might be, regardless of how much zeal or how much faith you might have. You must realize that you did not bring yourself to this study, but that Something impelled you, and the Something that impelled you is within you. Always the impulse comes from within.

A great responsibility rests upon those who go into the spiritual healing ministry, and of them is demanded the highest understanding. They will bring the richest blessings to mankind, but they will have heaped upon them all the villification that the human world can hurl at them. No one should go into this spiritual ministry unless God takes him by the nape of the neck and pushes him into it; and even then, if he can resist the call, he should do so. The spiritual ministry is not his place—it is no place for anyone—unless that inner Something insists, "There is just no other way."

All the spiritual courage a person can muster is required to withstand the antagonism the world has for truth and toward those who hold fast to truth. It does not lie within anyone's capacity as a human being to obey a spiritual call, except in proportion as the grace of God is laid upon him because only then can he have that greater light which is necessary.

The practitioner or teacher becomes a transparency for God-activity. It is his function to maintain such an awareness of truth that, when a student or patient comes to the consciousness of that practitioner, he will find nothing there but truth and love. For example, if a person brought himself to a practitioner whose consciousness has become a transparency for spiritual wisdom, he would so feel that spiritual activity as to settle down into a state of peace and wholeness. In proportion as a practitioner keeps himself filled with ideas of truth and love, inharmony and discord are eliminated from the experience of those who turn to him for help; and even those who pass him on the street, will, in the degree in which they are reaching out, partake of his consciousness because there is a continuous realization:

Since God is my consciousness, and God, or Truth, fills my consciousness and is the substance and activity of it, that Truth is the substance of the form *of everything within my universe, even if it appears as a tree or a flower, an enemy or a friend. Everything in my universe responds to that awareness.*

I embrace my universe within my consciousness, a universe formed of, and by, that consciousness; and because my consciousness is filled with Truth, my universe manifests the activity, quality, and substance, the nature and the character of Truth, of eternality and immortality.

I stand at the doorway of my consciousness, permitting nothing of a discordant nature to enter, maintaining it in its purity as that place through which God flows to all the world. All who enter my spiritual household, my temple, find therein the peace and joy which become the substance of their being, their bodies, or their pocketbooks. This God-consciousness envelops them, governs and sustains them, and reveals this truth as the truth of their own individual being, so that they, in their turn, become a law not only to themselves but to all who look to them for help.

Consciousness, imbued with truth, rooted and grounded in truth, will do the healing works, whether that consciousness is yours or mine. Everything in your world takes on the complexion of your consciousness, and any degree of inharmony and discord in your world is a reflection of the degree to which world beliefs have been permitted to get past the door of your consciousness. Do you not see, then, how you become a law unto your universe in proportion as the Christ-consciousness takes over your life?

Every time that an evidence of discord presents itself to you, you must reinterpret it until that conscious reinterpretation becomes a habit, and there is no longer any process involved. Whenever anyone asks for help, at least for a year or two or three, you should be willing to give the very best treatment you know how to give. But after a year or two of giving hundreds and hundreds, perhaps even thousands of treatments, the truth becomes so embedded and embodied in your consciousness and you are living in such a high state of consciousness that when somebody asks for help you are able simply to respond with, "I am with you," and this will be sufficient treatment. But that will only be possible after you have given enough treatments to have established yourself in the full realization of the truth.

The question is often asked, "What prevents a healing? Why is the truth not always effective or operative? Why does it take so long in some cases?" There are a dozen different answers, none of them entirely satisfactory. One is that the practitioner may not at that moment have risen to a high enough state of consciousness. In some cases when the disciples had failed to heal, the Master said, "This kind goeth not out but by prayer and fasting," which leads us to believe that there is a type of claim which does not respond to the ordinary treatment. Something higher is required, something of which only Jesus himself was the master.

You will find that there are claims that yield to the practitioner working on the spiritual level that will not yield to a practitioner working on the mental level. There are people who do not receive healings from medicine, and yet when those same people find a mental science practitioner, they respond very quickly. But on the other hand, there are many people who do not respond to mental treatment and find help only from a practitioner who works on the spiritual plane. Each individual must go within himself and, if he is sincere, he will be led to the practitioner who can meet his need.

Sometimes the practitioner even on the spiritual plane will fail to meet certain cases, and while that may have to do with the fact that he may not at that moment be on a high enough level of spirituality, it may also be that the patient is not yet ready to yield, to give up his material sense of existence or whatever is the nature of that state of consciousness that is binding him to the claim. Sometimes the practitioner's work will compel the patient to yield, but at other times he will cling to some state of consciousness which makes it well-nigh impossible for him to be healed.

There is more to healing than merely the restoration of physical well-being in the body. Sometimes it is much more important that the individual be spiritually awakened than that he have merely a physical healing. In that event, the practitioner may not be able to help him until this occurs, but after that the healing often follows quickly. It is the practitioner's responsibility to continue until the individual awakens, but *it is not the practitioner who awakens him: The Christ, through the practitioner's recognition of truth, awakens him.*

Many treatments are not effective for the simple reason that they are not clean-cut realizations of the truth of being. People make statements of truth, but they are fuzzy about them, and many times their statements are contradictory. A spiritual healer must be as clean-cut in his realization of truth as a musician or mathematician is in his understanding of music or mathematics. One little bit of fuzziness in mathematics results in the wrong answer; one little bit of fuzziness in music, and the wrong note is struck. So also it is vitally important to have a sharp and clear understanding of what the principles of spiritual healing are in order to make treatment effective.

Your consciousness of truth will be a law of harmony to your universe, provided it is a clearly defined consciousness; but if it is a fuzzy one, then there will be a fuzzy demonstration because you have applied only a fuzzy or inaccurate concept of law to the situation. The demonstration of harmony is not something for which you can sit idly by and wait: You must do something specific about it, and that something is to maintain the truth of being as the activity of your consciousness.

The practitioner becomes a law of harmony unto his patients in proportion to the truth he maintains in his consciousness; but if he allows thoughts of the world to occupy his attention or if he indulges in a personal sense of "I," "me," or "mine," he will not succeed in his spiritual ministry. A practitioner must come out and be separate. Especially must he rise high in spiritual integrity because people are entrusting him with the destiny of their souls at a particular stage of their unfoldment. That is a very sacred trust, and to keep it inviolate, the entire world must be given up so that he can live and move and have his being morning, noon, and night in the divine Consciousness.

Practitioners who are deeply involved in the duties of community or family life can seldom be successful because the needs of their patients and students must take precedence over all other obligations. Only what little time is left after they have discharged the responsibilities of their practice and ministry remains for their families. There is no room in a spiritual ministry for time-consuming social activities; there is no room left for many friends, nor for active participation in community or political life, although no practitioner should ever shirk his duty as a responsible citizen of his community, his nation, and of the world.

When a person enters the healing ministry, he must in large measure separate himself from his human contacts in order to hold himself in such a state of spiritual awareness that he is always ready for any and every call made upon him. This life is the life of the Soul, and it necessitates a death to the things of the world.

Just as the practitioner must not permit his personal relationships—family or social—to encroach upon his time in such a way as to pull him down from a high level of consciousness, so he must also guard against similar encroachments on the part of his patients or student-body. As long as I have been in this work, I have made it a rule that telephone calls be limited to about three minutes. The reason for that time limitation is so that others who call will find the line open and that my consciousness will not be cluttered with nonessentials.

A practitioner must at all times stand in readiness to accept calls whether day or night. There are no office hours in spiritual healing—except twenty-four hours a day, seven days a week. That does not mean that a practitioner should allow himself to be called out at all hours of the day or night to make personal visitations, except in exceptional cases. Why should he rush to a patient's side if the problem is only an illusion? If a practitioner is tempted to hurry to a patient's home because of the apparently urgent nature of the call, by his very action, he is accepting the appearance, and the case may be lost.

On rare occasions, it is permissible to call upon a patient personally, but under most circumstances the wisest course is for the practitioner to sit at home, live his life in God, always remaining steadfast in spiritual consciousness and never permitting the fears of the world to upset him. If the practitioner permits himself to accept appearances at face value, then he will be the blind leading the blind, and they will both fall into a ditch. Practitioners must hold themselves aloof from the world. This is not ignoring error; it is relegating error to its rightful place as nothingness: nothing to be feared, nothing to be hated, nothing to be loved—*nothing*.

Spiritual healing is accomplished only by an actual God-realization. It has nothing to do with the names of people or with the names of a disease or condition: It has to do with knowing the true identity of those who are appearing to you as patients. As a practitioner, you have no right to be interested in the name of the patient, the name of the disease, or its diagnosis; although no practitioner worthy of the name would ever fail to express kindness, love, and compassion to all those who come to him with their problems. He listens understandingly, but he does not hear because he knows that the all-knowing infinite Wisdom which is the reality of being knows everything, and It does not have to be told the name of the person or the name of the disease: It is an infinite intelligence which knows the need before you know it and before your patient does.

If a person tells you, "I have a headache," there is nothing you, humanly, can do about it; or if he says, "I have a footache," you can do no more about that. The same is true if he informs you it is a broken bone or consumption or cancer. What can you do about any of these things humanly? What good is that information to you? What is accomplished by all this listening to "rumors"? Why permit yourself to accept all these temptations to believe in a selfhood or a law apart from God, temptations which are all too eagerly thrust upon you by a loquacious patient?

The practitioner is far better able to remain in his consciousness of God if he pays no attention to the person, condition, or thing, but instantly realizes, "This person is a victim of a universal belief from which at the moment he does not know how to extricate himself."

If you have any expectation of being a part of a spiritual healing ministry, learn first of all never to condemn those whom you would help. Stop condemning; stop criticizing; stop judging. "Judge not after appearances." Lift yourself out of the mesmerism which indulges in condemnation. Everyone has faults and no one is proud of them. No one desires to perpetuate them, and yet that is the very thing you do if you continue to criticize, judge, or condemn yourself or others. Your function as a practitioner is never to hold an individual in bondage to any of his sins of omission or commission. Even if he commits them seventy times seven, still you must release him seventy times seven.

There must be understanding on the part of the practitioner; there must be compassion; there must be love; and that means understanding and compassion whether the patient is sinning or sick. In the degree that you can live and behold those about you without condemnation, always maintaining the attitude of "Neither do I condemn thee," do you lift yourself and others from the burden of their errors, and that sets you and them free to receive God's grace.

In this way, the condemnation of mortality is lifted from yourself and others, and man is revealed as the very image and likeness of God. That likeness constitutes your being and mine; it is the being of every saint who has ever lived, and of every sinner. The Master came that sinners might be redeemed even more than that good people might be made a little better. No sinner is ever cast out eternally;

no sinner is ever without redemption. One of the great functions of the Christ is to redeem, to restore, and to regenerate that which is lost, whether it is the lost crops, the lost years of the locusts, the lost health, or the lost morals. There could be no physical healing, if there were not also spiritual regeneration. When you restore one, you restore the other. They are both part and parcel of one whole.

If you hold man in condemnation to his faults, you will push him further down into the ground where he will never have an opportunity to rise up into wholeness of Spirit, mind, and body. Look into your patient's or student's heart and mind, and there find God enthroned. Until you can see that the person standing before you is God made manifest, you will be looking for God to do something for somebody, and that will defeat your purpose. Every time you are led to believe that your patient needs help, your spiritual vision is blurred. It is blurred in exactly the same way as was that of the man who was sitting at a bar with a friend drinking and who turned to the other chiding him, "You had better stop drinking; your face is getting blurred." So it is that every time you direct your treatment to somebody "out here," it is not the patient's face that is blurred or his body that is sick: It is your vision, your spiritual vision, that is blurred because it is you who are seeing the other person incorrectly.

Some of your patients will give you a hard battle before they yield, but do not be ensnared by any such resistance and be led to conclude that they are a little too wicked or a little too materialistic or a little too unloving. Do not be trapped into judging by appearances. You prove your readiness for God's ministry by being able to look any and every appearance in the face without judgment. Even if you have to continue looking at it for years, keep right on realizing:

Thou art the Christ of God. Thou art pure spiritual being. Christ sits enthroned in thy being. Thy mind is an instrument for God; thy body is the very temple of God. God is the Soul of thy being.

Do not forget to take into consideration all three parts of your patient's being—the Spirit or Soul, the mind, and the body. First of all, understand God to be the Soul, the Spirit, and the life of all being. Realize that the mind of every individual is an instrument through which God functions and that the body is the temple of the living God. Then you are beholding a whole man—Spirit, mind, and body—all one, all parts of the whole, and that Whole is God.

The practitioner is an instrument through which the voice of God utters Itself, and His word is quick and sharp and powerful. Let nobody believe that his own word is quick and sharp and powerful because nobody has risen to that point yet. Even Jesus Christ said quite unashamedly and with true humility, "I can of mine own self do nothing."

The practitioner must never be so puffed up with self-importance as to assume the duties or functions of God and think that he knows what is right for his patient or can tell him what is right or explain how he can bring harmony into his patient's experience. It is not the prerogative of the practitioner to enter the human scene with his human judgment and attempt to decide how a problem should be resolved. It is not the practitioner's wisdom that heals the patient, but *His* power, the power of God. Therefore, the function of the spiritual healer is to pray: He must become receptive and responsive, become a transparency, and then He comes whose right it is—quick and sharp and powerful—changing the body in the twinkling of an eye.

If the metaphysical teaching of the last century has proved anything at all, it is that any person who seriously wants to be a healer can become one—not easily always. To some that consciousness comes very quickly, to others slowly; but it is obtainable by anybody who is determined enough to have it. It has nothing to do with any mysterious outside God; it has nothing to do with any mysterious outside powers: It has to do with the degree of developed spiritual consciousness of the individual.

CHAPTER VIII

TREATMENT IS A REALIZATION OF OMNIPRESENCE

Many people are puzzled as to how the patient, rather than one hundred million other people, receives the benefit of a treatment if it is not necessary to know his name or his condition and if neither of these is taken into a treatment. The answer is found in the basic principle of oneness. The particular patient who has asked for help receives that help because he has reached out to the consciousness of the practitioner who understands that there is not a patient-consciousness, a practitioner-consciousness, *and* a God-consciousness: There is only one Consciousness—God-consciousness.

When a patient turns to a truly dedicated God-conscious practitioner, he makes himself a part of that practitioner's God-consciousness. Furthermore, a person may ask for help for his child, his parents, his pet poodle, or for his crops, and in so doing he brings them to the one infinite divine Consciousness which the practitioner is. Strangely enough, a person who does not bring himself to this Consciousness may sit with his ills in the same room right next to the practitioner year in and year out and receive no benefit.

Jesus walked up and down the Holy Land for three years, every day encountering the sick and the sinning, but only to those who came to him begging, "Master, Master, heal me," did he turn and say, "Do you believe that I can do this?"

Only those who brought themselves into the consciousness of the Master, only those who were a part of the multitude that sat at his feet, only they received the benediction of his great blessing.

Nearly everyone is surrounded with people who are in need of healing of one kind or another, and this poses the question as to what responsibility rests with a person regarding those who come within his orbit. Should treatment be withheld until help has been specifically requested? What about those in the world he sees around him who are in need of healing? Is he his brother's keeper? Such questions could not arise were this basic principle of treatment understood: No treatment is ever given to anyone or to any condition.

As you move about this world, inevitably aware of its frustrations and tragedies, you never treat anyone or any condition. Never! It is the claim that is presented to you that receives the treatment, and that claim is always the belief in a selfhood or condition separate and apart from God. Whenever any belief intrudes itself upon your thought, you must do something about it, not something to the person or the condition, but only to the claim as it presents itself to your thought.

When you see what looks like deformity, insanity, or an accident, go within; realize that this which you are witnessing is an illusion; feel the divine peace of God's presence. Every specific claim that presents itself to you has to be met in your consciousness—not only when people ask you for help, but whenever you observe a need. If you walk along the street and see an intoxicated person, that is a claim impinging on your consciousness, and it is in your consciousness that it must be met. If you see a crippled person or if you see a beggar, do not ignore him, do not pass him by; do not be like those who passed by the man on the road to Jericho and let him lie there. Do not you let him lie there—physically, you may pass him by, but spiritually lift him right up to the truth of being.

Some years ago in Honolulu, a young woman in one of our classes who was taking a bus home had her attention attracted to a man at the rear of the bus, very boisterous and obscene in his language. She immediately began to realize that God was manifest as individual being, that each individual includes all that God is, and that individual being has only the qualities of God. She did not treat the man; she did not know the truth about the man or the condition. She began with herself, and finally he came over and said, "Thank you, Miss, for praying for me. I'm all right now."

You cannot pass by or ignore people who are sick, sinful, or dying; you cannot evade your responsibility to lift them up in your consciousness through the realization of the infinite nature of God appearing as individual being. If there is any degree of receptivity, they will feel it. That is how you bless your neighbor as yourself and pray for your enemy. Your enemy is never a person; your enemy is always an appearance—every appearance of sin, disease, discord, lack, and limitation. There is only one way to pray, and that is to ask yourself, "Do I believe my eyes or do I believe the mystics of the world, those people who have had an intuitive contact with God and who have had the revelation that evil does not exist as a reality and that there is no law of sin or disease?"

Many people feel that they would like to give, or have treatments given, to their children, husbands, wives, and friends who are not even interested in spiritual healing, who are not on the spiritual path, and who have no desire to be on it. Despite their lack of interest, their well-meaning metaphysical friend or relative reaches out to help them because he loves them so much that he wants to see them free, and in his zeal he thinks he has the power to do it.

It cannot be emphasized too strongly, however, that every individual has the right to his own life and the right to his own death; he has the right to be healthy and he has just as much right to be sick; he has as much right to seek his health through *materia medica* as any other person has to seek his through God. The medically minded person does not relish having truth thrust down his throat by his metaphysical friends any more than does the one who seeks his health and harmony through spiritual wisdom or truth like to have his friends or members of his family interfering with him and attempting to dissuade him from his course.

Therefore, the person who believes in and practices spiritual healing must be extremely careful that he accords to all others the same freedom which he desires for himself. "All things whatsoever ye would that men should do to you, do ye even so to them"; and if anyone wants to use medicine, surgery, or any other form of material aid, he has a right to it, and he should be set free to find his good in his own way.

In cases where one person's demonstration affects another's, where a parent, husband, wife, or child is involved, it is not only the right, but the duty and privilege of the metaphysical student to know the truth and attain his own peace through a realization of God. Whether or not it frees those close to him is another thing—sometimes it does, and sometimes it does not. Sometimes it opens up in them a desire for freedom, even for spiritual freedom, but whether or not it does that, by abiding in the truth, he has done all that he can do. Always there must be a measure of receptivity before a person can receive help—that grain of faith, that "Do you believe that this can be done?"

All treatment is individual, but as has already been explained, the name, face, body, or anything which would identify the patient or disease does not enter the thought of the practitioner of spiritual healing. However, if a person telephones a practitioner to the effect that he is suffering from influenza, the treatment might be specific to the extent of dealing with the belief of infection or contagion or the world belief of weather or climate, but not in the sense of thinking specifically of the patient or the disease.

If a call came relaying the circumstances of an accident,

a practitioner might well realize in his treatment that God maintains law and order and sustains every idea in divine Consciousness, and that nothing ever has or will escape from the harmony, order, and law of that divine Consciousness. To that extent he would be specific, but never would he be specific to the extent of treating a broken leg or arm, or a pain whether on the right side or the left side, up or down. A person might have a pain in the region of the heart and yet not have heart trouble at all. Would it not be foolish then to attempt to treat the heart?

It would make no difference if three or three hundred people asked for help the same day, the process would always be the same. The moment an individual asks for help, that is when he, and nobody else, receives the treatment. No practitioner can make a list of names and think, "I am going to give all these people a treatment tonight." Actually, the treatment must be given the very moment a patient comes to his thought, whether that is by telephone, letter, telegraph, or whether suddenly the thought of the patient comes into his mind. At that instant, the treatment takes place, and not one minute later.

If somebody should come into my thought this very minute while I am writing this book, he would receive a treatment immediately. I would not dare to wait even one minute to give the treatment because there is only one time to correct the belief and that is when it comes to me. That is the time for the reinterpretation, or unfoldment. *The secret of healing is in reaction—in this immediate reinterpretation.*

There are practitioners who keep lists of patients, and they go through that list giving treatments when they get up in the morning and when they go to bed at night. Why do they do this? Why should it be necessary to go through a list of names, giving treatments, if the treatment is given when the call comes to them? The work should have been done at that time, unless the practitioner has been specifically asked again for help.

It is the obligation of a practitioner to stand by with a case and to continue his work until he has achieved a feeling of release or until the patient has asked him to discontinue the work. It is the function of the practitioner to give the patient help, but after he has given it and has felt a sense of release, he must assume that the burden is on God's shoulder and that it has been taken care of. Unless it comes back to his thought or unless he is asked for help again, he should drop the case.

It is not as if the practitioner were really trying to heal something when he is asked for help. The help he is expected to give is the realization that such conditions do not exist as reality. That is the reason he does not have to feel under the necessity of giving another treatment tomorrow. If the error does not exist today, it should not exist tomorrow, and, furthermore, any error which does not exist today could not have existed yesterday.

That is the reason why people at great distances frequently receive their help before I receive their request for help. Every day I remind myself that any error that is not true today was not true yesterday, and if it were not true yesterday, it was not true at the time the request for help was sent. I live always in the realization that this is the only moment, and the harmony that exists this moment is an eternal harmony which has always existed and always will exist. As I abide in that, everyone who reaches out to me for help must receive it, and he must receive it at the moment that he reaches out, since that is when I am knowing the truth.

When a practitioner awakens in the morning, he should not have a single patient unless he receives a call for help that very morning. Why should he, if he took care of the case at the moment the call came? Throughout the years of my practice, I have handled many, many cases a day. One year I averaged 135 calls a day, seven days a week, and never did I have a list of patients to treat. When a letter came the help was given and the person and the problem forgotten unless it came back to mind or unless he wrote again.

When a call for help comes, I take the position that "this is the day the Lord hath made," and this is the moment in which I do the work. If the patient drops from thought that is the end of it, but if he keeps returning to my thought, each time the treatment will be the highest I know.

Every day, however, I do what might be considered group work because, morning and night, I realize that anyone—anywhere or any time—reaching out to my consciousness does not have to wait to communicate with me personally, but that he must receive his answer instantaneously. All that is necessary is to reach out, and the answer will come.

This type of work is not group treatment in the commonly accepted sense of the term. However it might be called that, inasmuch as I am not thinking of any specific individual, not of thirty, forty, or a hundred individual people, but of a patient-body or a student-body. In going into meditation for such a group, which I do many, many times a day, I would not take forty or a hundred different people into consciousness. I would merely know that as a group, they are not affected by world beliefs or suggestions.

From then on, the group would not come into my meditation: My meditation would be wholly centered on God and the principle involved, which is that God is the consciousness of individual being. In that divine Consciousness, there are no laws of matter, no laws of weather; no beliefs operate in the mind which is the instrument of Consciousness, or God. There is only one Presence, one Power, one Consciousness, and that God-consciousness is the consciousness of the group.

It is through such daily meditation periods, in which many of us in The Infinite Way embrace in our consciousness all of our students, that our world-wide student-body is maintained relatively free of world mesmerism, and thereby sin, disease, lack, and other human discords are lessened in their experience.

There might also be times when I would be thinking of my family, not of each member specifically, but of the family as a unit. Then I would meditate in the same way as I would for one of our Infinite Way classes, knowing that God constitutes the mind, the life, and the Soul of my family. Nothing can enter from without to create discord or inharmony because all law and government are from within—from the divine Consciousness which is the life of the individual and of the family.

If I were a teacher in a schoolroom, in a Sunday school, or if I were the minister of a church, that is how I would meditate. In the first place, I would go into meditation because of the class or congregation, but then I would immediately dismiss them from consciousness and rise into the realization that since God is the church-consciousness, and God is the consciousness of every individual who constitutes the church, only one law is operating in that classroom or church. The government is on His shoulders.

The only other occasion for a group treatment might be in connection with the armed forces throughout the world. In such cases, no one individual would be singled out as if there were one truth about one person and a different truth about another, but God would be realized as the consciousness of everyone involved in the situation, and this must include the armies of the enemies as well as our own.

A good general rule to follow is not to attempt to give group treatments except in situations similar to those cited above. The only other time that group healing or the treating of many patients together is advisable is when a practitioner turns to God in a realization of conscious oneness for the sake of communion with God, but without any individual cases first entering thought. He is not dealing specifically with any of these cases, but whoever is reaching out to him will be healed, and perhaps even four or five during that period of meditation. The practitioner is not treating a group of patients: He is consciously one with God, and while he is in communion with God, all those who reach out and touch his consciousness at that moment find healing.

From many years of experience, I know that the degree of my upliftment determines the degree of harmony, peace, joy, prosperity, health, and wholeness of those who constitute my practice or student-body. To illustrate, in the early years of my practice, I was kept busy during the winter with many calls, sometimes hundreds, for the healing of influenza, colds, and pneumonia. Then one winter in New England, an experience took place which opened my consciousness to the depth of Jesus' statement, "I and my Father are one."

One evening I left the office after twenty-nine calls had come in during the afternoon from people in different stages of colds, grippe, and the "flu." The next morning, almost before I was seated in my office, there were six more calls. At that particular time, I was very busy, and, of course, every chair in my office waiting room was usually occupied, and my appointment book was always filled. On this day, however, when I looked at my appointment book, I found that there were no appointments scheduled for the hour from one to two, and that was something that had never before happened to me. Furthermore, I had not consciously or deliberately arranged it that way, so I wondered, "What has happened? What does this mean?"

Then in a flash it came to me, "Oh, I didn't do that. I had nothing to do with that. This must have been God's work. There must be a reason for this." And so I closed the office door just as if I were with a patient, sat down, and said, "Father, there is a meaning to this. Let me know what it is."

And then I waited in meditation until this came to me: "You do not have thirty-five cases of colds and the "flu": You have only one, and that one is the belief in a selfhood apart from God. It is a belief that there are powers operating in consciousness other than God. Can you accept any power

outside of God, the one Consciousness, the one divine Intelligence? Can you acknowledge that there is some power
operating outside of your own consciousness?"

That was a new idea. During the afternoon following that
revelation, there were no further calls relative to that particular type of problem. Every one, or very nearly every one,
of those patients, was healed during that hour of realization.
Just as soon as the truth of being registered in my consciousness, all these people were released. It was not a matter of
giving each one a treatment; it was not a matter of meditating for them or thinking about them: It was a matter of
the truth of being registering in my consciousness; and then
every one who had brought himself to my consciousness was
healed. If I am entertaining the truth of being, any one, any
thirty-five, or any three hundred who come to my consciousness partake of the nature of the truth operating in that
consciousness.

That is the way to treat; that is how to go about the
world being a blessing and a benediction. You do not treat
people and you do not try to realize the Christ in them:
You realize the Christ as the only being. Realize the Christ;
feel the Christ; feel the warmth of love within your own
being. Many of those you are silently blessing will have
healings, and some of them will find their way to truth because you will have opened up the spiritual center in them
which heretofore had not been open. "I, if I be lifted up
from the earth, will draw all men unto me."

PART THREE

SPIRITUAL
HEALING:

THE PRACTICE

WHAT ABOUT THIS BODY?

The principles of spiritual healing have been explained in the foregoing chapters, but an explanation does not heal. Even though you have gained some understanding of these principles, in order for them to be made practical and workable, and for you to develop a healing consciousness, they must be removed from the realm of generalities, from a mere intellectual exercise, and brought to bear on specific problems, whether financial, moral, mental, or physical.

One problem which is uppermost in the lives of a great many people is that of health, that of an ailing or aging body. Even those who are at the moment experiencing physical well-being are puzzled by the relationship of what they see as a material body to the spiritual scheme of things. What about this body? How does it fit into a spiritual universe? Is this material body the Word made flesh? Is it the material body or only the spiritual body which is resurrected? Does the material body manifest God?

Do not be too startled when I say to you that there is only one body: There is not a material body *and* a spiritual body. There is only one. Here, as in every aspect of life, the principle of oneness applies.

True, we entertain a *material concept* of body, and it is that concept of body which gets all twisted up and involves us in all manner of ills, but the body has no power to cause trouble; the body has no power to be good or bad, sick or well: *It is our concept* which appears as a sick or well body.

When your concept is a material sense of body, you open yourself to all the sins and diseases to which the body may be subject. The moment, however, that you drop that concept and realize that there are not two or three or four kinds of bodies, but that there is only one body, and that body is the temple of the living God, God-governed, God-maintained, and subject only to the laws of God, you bring this very body under God's grace. If you believe that your body is material, you are limiting yourself; but if you feel, "Well, as I see it, I certainly have a material *sense* of it," I can understand that and agree with you because everybody to some degree entertains a material sense of body.

Jesus carried a material sense of body with him right up to the Ascension. Even after the Crucifixion when he walked the earth, he still had the marks of the nails and the sword in his side, showing that even at that advanced stage of spiritual unfoldment he was entertaining in some measure a material sense of body, although far less than any other person of whom there is any knowledge. It was only at the Ascension that he rose, not above the physical body, not above a material body, but above *a material sense* of body. Then what became of his wounds and blood? They were not there: He had become pure white essence, so white in essence that he ascended out of sight.

When you can arrive at an understanding that even though you are entertaining a material sense of body you are not a material body, gradually the material sense of body will dissolve in the realization that there is no power in effect, no power in the body, no power in the organs and functions of the body, no power in germs, no power in food. "All power is given unto me."

Then you are not well because your heart is well: Your heart is well because you exist. You do not walk because your legs are harmonious: Your legs walk because you are harmonious. In physical health, you are only healthy because your body is healthy; but spiritually when you are whole, your wholeness governs the activity of your body. There fore, your body does not govern your health; it is your health that governs your body. It is you who govern your body through the realization of your true identity, and that realiza tion becomes the health of all those who turn to you.

Let us assume that John Jones has asked for help for a physical condition. He may have mentioned that his problem was influenza, which at that time was raging throughout his community and may have reached almost epidemic proportions. In your treatment, your first recognition is that this is a suggestion of a selfhood apart from God, and that leaves you free to forget the patient and the condition. The entire truth that you know is about God, and the entire treatment remains on the level of God:

If God is infinite being, there is no other being; there is no John Jones-being separate and apart from God. There cannot be God as infinite being and some other being besides God. God is an all-inclusive good and besides that Good there is nothing else.

Furthermore, if God is infinite, God must include all law and be the only law. That eliminates all possibility of any law other than the law of God. Therefore, in the spiritual kingdom, no laws of matter can operate; in that Kingdom, there can be no law of infection or contagion; there can be no laws of material evil: There is only God-law, spiritual law—perfect, complete, harmonious, all-enforcing, and self-enforcing. There is nothing to oppose the law of God, nothing to contend against it. God alone is law.

God is the only life, the life of individual you and me. The life of God can never be sick or weakened, nor can it be subject to external influences of any nature other than God.

Your entire treatment is kept in the realm of God, in the realization of God as individual life, individual mind, individual law, Spirit, substance, and of God as the only cause. If God is the only cause, God must be the only effect; and if God is the only effect, that ends the treatment right there. You have nothing to meet now but God—God as Cause, God as Effect, God as Life, God as Law, God as all true Being.

By means of the first half of this treatment, you have lifted yourself above fear and above the appearance. The appearance was a John Jones with a claim of the "flu," but by remaining in the realm of God's completeness, you have long since lost any thought of John Jones and his problem. You are now tabernacling with God and his angels. You have come to the end of your part of the treatment, and you now take the attitude of listening as if you really expected to hear a voice.

Sooner or later there comes a deep breath, a "click," sometimes a message, but usually something of a nature that brings release. The responsibility is gone and now rests on His shoulders. That ends the treatment as far as you are concerned, and you can now dismiss it because God is on the field, and it is no longer your responsibility.

Six or eight or twelve hours later, John Jones may call and report, "I am feeling worse," or "I am feeling better," or "I am completely free." If he is completely free, that is the end of it. But if he is worse or if he is just the same or feeling some better, you may feel led to give him another treatment. And so you will go back again, not in the same words or thoughts, but always keeping your conversation in heaven, always keeping your treatment on the level of God. Realize the truth only about God because any truth you know about God is the truth about you or me or John Jones. That is a natural corollary of the infinity of God. God is infinite, and, therefore, there is no you or me or John Jones except as, in, and of the Godhead. No one can be outside of God if God is infinite, and being a part of and in God, whatever truth is known about God is the truth about individual being.

In almost every case that comes to you, you will find some human or material sense of law operating: It may be a law of infection or contagion, or a law of decomposition or breakage. Always some kind of a law has been laid down humanly, and that must be recognized as but of the substance of hypnotism.

The problem may be one of organic or functional disease, and then into the treatment might come the realization that just as the leaves and stem do not govern the life of a plant but that life governs it, so the organs and functions of the body do not govern life: Life governs the organs and functions of the body. As long as life is flowing, the plant flourishes; the stem and leaves are but the outer expression of the life-force.

In the same way, it is not the heart, the liver, or the lungs which determine life. God is life, and that life cannot be affected by the organs and functions of the body. Therefore, you do not have to be concerned whether they act in accordance with laws laid down by *materia medica*. By reversing these laws and realizing that life governs every activity of the body, it will manifest harmony and painlessness. In this realization of the true government of the body, you do not come down to the level of the body. You have merely corrected the belief that the body affects life by the understanding that life governs the body. The heart could not beat without life beating it; the digestive or eliminative organs could not work if there were not an intelligence and a life permeating those organs and acting in, on, and through them.

The organs and functions of the body should not be feared: They do not have within them the power of destruction, death, or disease, because inherent in every person is the power of God which is a resurrection even to the dead body, the dead organ, the dead function, or the dead muscle. Within individual consciousness is the power of resurrection.

The Word becomes flesh. Does It change Its nature in

becoming flesh? No, not any more than water changes its nature when it becomes ice or when it becomes steam; in either form, it still has the properties of water. So it is that as the Word, God, becomes flesh, It does not change Its nature; It remains the Self-created, Self-maintaining substance, containing within Itself the law, the cause, and the activity of Its form.

The realization of God as the governing principle of all there is, of God as the only substance and the only law, dissolves the appearances which the world calls sickness, sin, fear, and death. When you are living from the standpoint of concepts or beliefs, your experience is the manifestation of those beliefs; but the activity of truth in consciousness is the word of God made flesh as harmonious being.

Even though this is not always easy to do, and despite the temptation to dwell on the appearance, recognize it as suggestion, or hypnotism, and turn immediately to God: Keep your treatment up in that circle called God and let your knowing be the truth about God. There is no truth about a physical body because it is only a concept. *God is the animating principle or law of all that is.* Do not pass over that statement too lightly because daily and hourly you will encounter the laws of "this world." Your treatment is that God is law:

God, being infinite, law is infinite. Therefore, the only law that there can be is a spiritual law, and that spiritual law is the only law operative in individual experience, animating being and body. There is no physical law, mental law, or moral law to be overcome. I recognize only one law, and that is the infinite law of God, eternally and infinitely omnipresent. The law which is God is the all-power; It does not have to contend with other laws. It is itself the only law and the all-law, a spiritual law, besides which there are no material laws, no moral laws, no mental laws, and no physical laws. There is only one law and that law is God.

Do not try to overcome material law, mental law, moral law—any law. Always recognize that you are dealing with but one law. Anything to the contrary that may be there is but a *material sense* of law. As you recognize spiritual law as the only law, all other claims of law disappear.

The moment a problem of any nature is presented immediately bring to consciousness the nature of the claim as material sense, or hypnotism. Then the word God must come into consciousness simultaneously so as to blot out the entire picture of people, conditions, or circumstances.

I remember a call that came from someone who had fallen afoul of a patch of poison ivy and was displaying the usual symptoms from having gotten into such a predicament. Quickly it came, so quickly that it was not a conscious thought, that since God made all that was made, God was the constituent element or property of all that existed, and therefore, the only effect could be something consonant with the nature of God.

According to appearances and according to human belief, there are properties that are unlike the good we associate with God; and there is no use denying that, because insofar as the human picture is concerned it is quite obvious. However, in The Infinite Way, you are not dealing with appearances. The very essence of treatment in this teaching is: "Judge not according to the appearance, but judge righteous judgment." If you judge after appearances, you will be involved with the powers of this world.

Do not deny the appearance of physical discord, but acknowledge God as the substance of all form. God is always appearing as the substance of form whether that form appears as a rosebush or as poison ivy. Unless you have trained yourself by persistent practice in looking through the appearance, you may find it difficult to realize that God is the animating principle of everything that exists. The appearance may be called poison ivy, a rose, or a tumor, *but there is no "it."* The truth is that God is the substance and law of all that is.

When you can see through the appearance to God as the substance of the form, you will not be afraid to look at either poison ivy or tumors, because then you will understand that these are but a misinterpretation of that indestructible substance which is untouched by sin, disease, fear, worry, hate, envy, jealousy, or malice. This indestructible substance contains within itself the power of self-creation and self-maintenance. Make it a matter of daily realization:

My body has neither qualities nor quantities of good or of evil. It has neither sickness nor health, is neither large nor small, has neither life nor death: My body is the temple of God, God-substance expressed as form and embodying and including all the qualities and quantities which constitute God, the I Am, the Soul. My body has neither youth nor age: It is as ancient as God and as young as each new day.

My body is not governed by laws of matter or of mind, but by the grace of God, for "thine is the kingdom and the power, and the glory." God is the light of my body. In my body is neither material darkness nor mental ignorance, for God is the light unto His holy temple, which my body is. God unfolds, discloses, and reveals Himself as body—as temple, a place of holiness and peace. God's grace maintains and sustains His body, which my body is.

CHAPTER X

SPIRITUAL UNFOLDMENT—
NOT HUMAN BIRTH OR DEATH

In God's creation, there was light before there was a sun. In God's creation, there was a crop before there was a seed planted. In other words, there were no material processes. That is the secret of Melchizedek: Melchizedek had neither father nor mother—no physical process was involved in his coming into being. Do you not know that that is the true life of you and of me? Do you not know that, in our true identity, we are Melchizedek, having neither mother nor father? "Call no man your father upon the earth: for one is your Father, which is in heaven."

In the Adam-dream, there is incarnation after incarnation, but in our true identity, there is no process of birth or death: There is always the *I*:

I stand back of me, and I know all that is happening to this person called "me," and to this thing called "my body." But I am not identified with it. I am here, and I was here before I was conceived in my mother's womb, and I will be here if I should ever go through the experience of passing on. I will be out here witnessing it. It will be an experience that will be happening to my body, but not to the I, just as my birth was not to the I of me.

I know that I am I, and I know that I took this form, transforming it from childhood to youth, youth to manhood, young manhood to maturity; and I know that this transform-

ing process will continue until one of these days I shall evolve out of this sense of body into whatever the true identity or form of my body may be, because there is an I, and I am that I. I stand here as a witness.

I am aware of myself as a person; I am aware of my body. I am aware of you as a person; I am aware that you as a person have a body, and in most cases I am aware of your true identity, I can almost feel the reality of you which lies behind your eyes: That is you; that is where you are. This other thing out here is only the form that you have assumed in this experience for the purpose of expression.

Child-conceiving and child-bearing are only concepts of human belief. What is called the conception and birth of a child is, in reality, God unfolding, disclosing, and revealing Itself. In dealing with cases of unborn children or newly born children, frequently the very first thing that comes to me is that in all this world there is no such thing as a child. To the uninitiated, this may seem like a very strange and startling statement to make, but stop and think for a moment. God is always at the point of absolute maturity; God is always at the point of complete perfection. If you had a developed spiritual vision, you would know that the harvest is already complete before the seed is in the ground. So it is with a child.

You may quite naturally ask, "Why, then, do we see a person develop—grow from infancy to maturity and from maturity to old age?" What we are witnessing is the unfolding of our concept of human birth, growth, and maturity, not the birth or growth of spiritual being, the Son of God. It is like watching a moving picture that is already complete on the roll of film. We watch it as it unrolls in time and space from beginning to end. But remember that that film we are witnessing was a complete picture before it was shown on the screen: It merely unfolded in time and space to our view.

So it is that the maturing of an infant is an activity of God unfolding in time and space. Actually, it was complete from the beginning; it had its full maturity, its complete being in the beginning—always had it, always has it, and always will have it. Such a realization as this is a treatment to all cases of unborn children and newly born children. God cannot be conceived; God cannot be born: Neither the life of God, the mind of God, nor the Soul of God can be conceived: It can only unfold as individual being.

In the human realm, there is the seed of the male and the female. No one really knows how those seeds are planted in every individual. And yet what could have planted them within every person but Life Itself? Are they not the product of Life? Life created those seeds, and Life functions through the seed so that it does not remain a seed forever. Through this activity of life the seeds change their forms, and in time these changing forms become living witnesses. Were the father and mother the creators of the child, or were they merely the avenues or instruments through which the child came into expression? Even from the human standpoint, there is a spiritual or invisible force behind creation which creates the seed.

If God is that force, then all that we can inherit is of the Father-Mother-God, the emanation of the one Life, one Life expressing Itself, one Life revealing Itself, one Life demonstrating Itself, one Life mainfesting Itself individually, universally, impersonally, and impartially. Certainly that individualization can have no quality that it does not receive from its Source. The qualities, nature, and character of God are made manifest in Its expression in individual life.

It is true that there is the appearance of humanhood; it is true that there is a claim of a selfhood apart from God. When a problem claiming to have its basis in heredity arises, ponder the idea of God, the one Life, and the nature of the divine heritage. Realize the divine heritage of man as Spirit, life, truth, love, harmony, joy, peace, power, and dominion.

Remember such scriptural truths as, "We are the children of God: And if children, then heirs; heirs of God, and joint-heirs with Christ." What then can be the nature of heredity except life and love?

Do you realize what it means to "Call no man your father upon the earth: for one is your Father, which is in heaven"? If you call no man on earth your father, you have only one parent: You have no parents on earth, so your parentage is not white or black or yellow, not Oriental or Occidental. Everyone has the same parent, and that parent is the Father in heaven, the one spiritual creative Principle. Each one is the son of God. That some are more educated than others, some more literate, or some more cultured is only an outer development created by environmental circumstances. There is but one Father, one creative Principle, and you are heir to all the heavenly riches. You are not anything of yourself, but by sonship, you are all that God is; you have all that God has, because "Son, thou art ever with me, and all that I have is thine."

As you attempt to apply this principle of divine sonship, you become aware of certain limitations in your experience and in the experience of those around you. Apparently everybody at some time or other experiences some kind of lack presumably due to heredity or to the accident of birth: lack of intelligence, lack of opportunity, lack of education, lack of economic security, or lack of an adequate vehicle of expression. But when you have pondered the meaning of this lesson until you are convinced of its truth, you will understand how to meet every appearance of limitation:

The five senses may testify to limitation, but I accept only the truth that I and the Father are one, and that all that the Father has is mine. I have accepted my divine sonship; I have accepted myself as an heir of God to all the heavenly riches—intelligence and unlimited opportunity. No good thing will He withhold from His beloved.

Ponder that; keep that in front of you. There may be days and weeks and months when limitation persists with unremitting force, but that is your testing time. Are you going to believe and accept the appearance or are you going to hold steadfastly to your conviction:

The divine child of God never knew, never knows, and never can know such a thing as limitation in any form. God is my Father. God is the creative principle, and the son is heir to all the intelligence and wisdom of the Father. God is the quality and the quantity of the son, His essence. I am of the family of God; I am an offspring of God, not of man.

The contemplation of the truth that you have no earthly parentage but that the Spirit of God is your creative principle sets you free from the limitations of humanhood. No longer do you move on the level of humanhood affected by the times and tides of human experience. You are lifted above that and ultimately you begin to discern the meaning of such spiritual relationships as the basic human relationship between parent and child.

Just as the message in this book is not mine, but comes through me as the instrument; so parents are the instruments through which their children come, and although parents are a necessary part of the picture in every person's human experience, they are not creators. God is the creator, and parents are the instruments through which God operates to bring His children to earth.

To acknowledge that the only life there is, is God, and that it is not subject to material beliefs is the way to maintain the life and vitality of your body in its absolute perfection. Then life is not subject to material conditions or to mental beliefs: It is subject only to Itself, which is God, the law and the life.

When you are in that circle called God, what do you see? Life. How old is life? Of how long a duration is that life? What is the nature of life? What do you know about life from the standpoint of spiritual vision?

Life is the word that will probably come to you more frequently than any other word when you are faced with a person who appears to be suffering from age or debility. Again you will ask, "What is the nature of life?" And the answer will come:

God is life; and in that life which is God there are no years. Life has within Itself the seed of Its own perpetuation. It has within Itself the law of continuity, immortality, eternality. This eternal, immortal life of God is fulfilled as individual being. There is no age to be dealt with because I do not have the life of man to improve or prolong: I have only the life of God to behold.

Do not fear this human sense of life or the loss of it. The human sense of life is not your real life. Your real life is the life you are living in your Soul. That is your life, your real being. The body is not the governor of that life, but that life governs the body. Life really is the animating principle of the body. The body does not influence you; you influence the body. The body is not a law unto your life; your life is a law unto your body. The body does not control consciousness; consciousness controls the body.

No religion or teaching, however, no matter how spiritual it is, keeps people on earth in sight of one another forever. All inevitably pass from human sight, but as they gain more enlightenment, this passing is not considered as a tragic experience because the illumined realize that it is not a part of a divine plan that anyone should remain on this plane and in this form for all time.

Just as you outgrew infancy and childhood, just as adulthood merged into the middle years, so will you outgrow this entire human experience, and unless you fight to cling to this present experience that transition should be a progressive step. Begin as soon as you can to look on the experience of passing, not with horror and not as if it were the end of something beautiful. It is not the end: It is the beginning. It is but the end of one phase of experience and the beginning of another.

You surely know that had life on earth been meant to be a continuous experience, the men who have contributed as much to life as have Abraham, Isaac, Jacob, Moses, Elijah, Elisha, Jesus, John, Paul, Krishna, Buddha, and Lao-tze would still be here visible to sight. But with all their understanding and with their great contribution to human welfare, each in his turn had to pass from human experience into a broader field of activity, and so will every human being.

Do not look upon healing work as if its object were solely to keep everybody here on earth permanently. That is not its object. Its object is spiritual regeneration so that as the Soul expands, each individual is ready for higher experiences, not only here on earth, but the higher experiences that can come to him as he leaves this earth. Never believe for a moment that any of these men that I have just named and countless others whom I could name are dead. Never believe that they are not now as much alive and present as they were when they were visible. Never doubt for a minute but that they are continuing their spiritual ministry, for it is they who are responsible for such spiritual progress as is being made today. It is the truth that they are throwing into consciousness; it is the truth they lived on earth and are still living that those on the spiritual path are catching glimpses of; and that is why the literature of these people lives on. As the Master said, "My words shall not pass away." Those who rise high enough in spiritual consciousness receive and accept these spiritual messages which are taken into consciousness through the written word.

Every time an impartation reaches you within, it comes from God, but is there a God separate and apart from His individualized form? No, God is forever expressing as individual you and me, and that expression continues on into eternity. Each one can discover this for himself by inner mystical experience, and he can find corroboration in the convincing accounts of the mystics of all ages. The mystics —the teachers and prophets of the Old as well as of the New Testament—have explained this in such a clear, simple manner that the message should never have been lost; but its very simplicity has blinded men and women to its significance: "I will never leave thee, nor forsake thee. . . . Before Abraham was, I am. . . . I am with you alway, even unto the end of the world."

Every scriptural promise in the Old Testament or in the New that relates to the word *I* is your assurance of immortality. How can you separate yourself from the *I* of your being? Birth has not separated you from it; death will not separate you from it, nor will accident. *I* did not begin with birth; *I* will not end with death, for *I* am with you since before Abraham. Jesus did not say that he would be with you: He said *I* is with you; he said, "Before Abraham was, I am" and "I am with you alway, even unto the end of the world." If he had said Jesus will be with you until the end of time, there would not have been a Christian religion today, because Jesus is not walking this earth today.

You, too, can say *I* and always find It there within yourself —find the *I* within yourself. When you are sick, you will find that *I* is there; when you come to your last moments, *I* will be there with you; and as you cross that borderline which is called death, *I* will carry you right across because *I*, your individual identity, can never be obliterated.

Once you have located God as the *I* of your being, your permanent identity, you have nothing to fear. If you make your bed in hell, *I* am there; if you walk through the valley of the shadow of death, *I* am there. You have nothing to fear as long as you consciously remember that *I* am with you. If you are lost in the desert, that *I* will set a table in the wilderness for you; It will lead you to an oasis; It will keep you harmoniously until you find that oasis and It will guide you to it—*I*, *I*, *I* will, *I* in the center of your being.

In the spiritual kingdom, there is no future tense. Just remember that one statement: In the spiritual kingdom, in the kingdom of God, in the kingdom of peace, joy, power, and dominion, there is no future tense. There is no such thing as time: There is only an eternal now, and in that eternal now, *I am.* To human sense, this may be a deathbed, or being lost in the desert, or being adrift on the ocean, or suffocating in a burning building. That is what the appearance may testify to, but the answer to it is *I—I am.* There is no future tense: You cannot be saved in the future, just as you cannot be saved in the past.

It makes no difference what the clock says or what the calendar says: It is still now and always will be now. And it is in this now that *I* in the midst of you am your salvation. The answer to every problem is the word *I* and the word "now." *I now am.* I now am about my Father's business. And what is my Father's business? To glorify God. You are only alive and well that God's glory can be manifest. That is the only reason you exist—that God's grace may be made visible.

Anyone who fears has no God. Fear is atheism. Fear is a conviction that there is no God. The minute you have a God, you cannot have fear. What would you fear? To go through the valley of the shadow of death? Why would you fear that? Is not everybody going to make an exit from this plane of consciousness some day? Has not every generation sent eighteen-, nineteen-, and twenty-year-old youngsters—boys and girls—out to get killed at the front? They were not afraid to do that to them. Why should they fear the same experience to which they have subjected these young people?

Passing from this scene is not death: It is only death to those who fear it, and they wake up to find out how unnecessary were their fears, and to discover that passing from this scene is but a transitional experience. Everybody has to go through it. Do you think that you or I will be the exception—that we shall be spared? Do you think that you and I are not going to go through that same experience? Never doubt that we shall, because it is not any more a part of God's plan for man to stay on earth forever than it is for him to stay a child forever or to stay thirty years of age forever. I suppose that if you or I were God, we would arrange it so that everybody would remain a glamorous or handsome thirty or thirty-five always. That would be our idea of an ideal world, but if this were true, I am sure that God would have planned it that way.

We live an eternal and an immortal life. Whether we are six years of age, sixty, or six hundred, we are still living. The body changes from the body of an infant to the body of a child, from the body of puberty to the body of adolescence, from the body of an adult to the body of what we call middle age, but it should never become the body of old age: It should always be the body of real maturity. Then would come that transitional experience of walking right out into our next phase of existence which is but a continuation of our work on this plane.

What is man's state of being when he passes from this world? One thing is certain, and that is that those who are not on the spiritual path will not be placed on that path just by the act of dying. It is safe to assume that they will be in the very same state of consciousness when they awaken as they were when they left here. But, and this I know not from assumption but from experience, those who are on the spiritual path, regardless of how little progress they seem to have made, are instantly, by the very act of passing, lifted into a higher atmosphere than they experienced here on earth. In other words, if they are on the spiritual path, the very act of passing is a release from a great deal of this material sense of existence. That does not mean jumping out of a window to attain that release because that would only be an increase of material sense. But the very act of passing, even when it is brought about through disease or accident, seems to release those who are on the spiritual path from much of the material sense of existence, and they instantly enter a higher consciousness.

The ultimate is that everyone eventually attain complete Christ-realization. How many days, weeks, months, years, or eons that will require, or how many times we shall have to return to the human sense of existence for another opportunity to learn, that perhaps knoweth no man.

One thing is certain: You did not choose to enter the spiritual path; you had no such power as a human being. As a matter of fact, as a human being, you might have rejected this way of life because the spiritual life will not enhance your *material* sense of good; it opens up a world of *spiritual* good. That is why people who believe that they can increase their physical health or material wealth through spiritual means have many lessons awaiting them, and perhaps the first of these is that they will increase their physical health and material wealth only in proportion as they drop these as aims and accept as their aim the desire for God-realization. It is true that these are added things, but that is not the goal. The goal of the spiritual life is to awaken in His image and likeness and to realize your spiritual identity as Christ, the Son of God.

CHAPTER XI

THE RELATIONSHIP OF ONENESS

Your world and mine is an outpicturing of our consciousness: When that consciousness is imbued with truth, our universe expresses harmony, orderliness, prosperity, joy, peace, power, and dominion; when there is an absence of truth in our consciousness—an acceptance of world values and world beliefs—then our world takes on the complexion of the chance, change, and luck characteristic of world belief. All conditions reflect the activity of the consciousness of the individuals concerned.

Your world is embodied in your consciousness; it reflects the state of your consciousness because your consciousness governs your world. Your awareness of truth is the law unto your world; but, on the other hand, your ignorance of truth likewise becomes a law unto it. For example, there is no law of darkness because you know that darkness can be dispelled by the presence of light. Yet in the absence of light, darkness would claim presence; and just so in the absence of truth in your consciousness, ignorance, lies, appearances, discords, and inharmony claim to be present. Therefore, in the absence of the activity of truth in your consciousness, your world will reflect chance, luck, human belief, medical belief, or astrological belief; but the activity of truth operating in and as your consciousness becomes a law of harmony unto everything in your world and makes everything concerning you reflect the harmony of your consciousness.

Suppose that you find yourself in a situation where you are faced with a roomful of people with whom you must work in some capacity or other—talk to them, instruct them, or serve them. As you look at them, they present a variety of appearances—good people, bad, sick, well, rich, and poor. How can you establish a sense of oneness with all these people? To feel a sense of union with any other person means, first of all, that you must make your contact with the Spirit within and find your own completeness; you must make your contact with the Father within, whereupon you automatically become one with every other individual within range of your consciousness.

This is your opportunity to apply the principles of The Infinite Way. Look over or through every person in the room to God:

God is the animating principle of every individual; God is the mind of every person here, the intelligence expressing as person. God is the only love, and God being infinite, God is all love; therefore, God is the love of individual being, and being filled with the love which is God, no individual can be used as an instrument for hate, envy, jealousy, or malice.

Realization such as that will lift you above personalities into the realm of pure being.

You may be confronted with evidences of misunderstanding, but what difference does it make what the appearance is? Right where that appearance is foisting itself upon your mind, God is. You are dealing only with God, not with beliefs, persons, or conditions.

Over and over again it has been proved that when confronting people who have fallen prey to anger or when meeting with vicious animals poised and ready to attack, by merely holding to the realization of God as the real entity or identity —the real being—God as the only law, the only substance, the only cause, the only effect, what we call healing takes place. This method of treatment never leaves the realm of

God, never comes down to the level of man or person or condition or circumstance, nor does it take unemployment, sin, or disease into consideration.

It is so easy to say that this is good and that is evil, this is of God and that is of the devil; but it is when a person or circumstance claims to have the power to crucify or set you free, to cause you trouble, to do this or that to you, that you must take your stand and realize:

My being is in Christ, and as long as I maintain my being in Christ, only the Christ can operate in my consciousness—which is the one consciousness, the consciousness of every person in the world.

In other words, when you look out at this world and see persons or circumstances claiming to have power over you for good or evil, you again must acknowledge that your being is in Christ and only the Christ-inspired can have any influence in your affairs.

Several years ago in a period of distress it came to me that I must love those who hate me, I must give love for ingratitude; and my answer was, "Father, I just can't do it. I don't know how to do it. Yes, I can be a hypocrite and say that I love these people who are hating, condemning, judging, and fighting me; but I can tell you truthfully that I don't—I don't know how to love them. It is true I have no antagonism toward them because I know what motivates them and I do not blame them. If I did not have a little understanding of Your infinite love, I might do the same thing in their position; so I have no sense of judgment or criticism or condemnation of them. I can even say, 'Father, forgive them; for they know not what they do'—but to love them! No, I cannot honestly say that I love them. I just cannot do that. If there is to be any loving, I am perfectly willing to be the avenue through which You, God, can love them through me. If that can be arranged, let's have it that way; but don't ask me to love them because that is beyond my capacity."

It was less than a minute after that that I settled down into a beautiful peace, went to sleep, and awakened completely healed. It is impossible to love ingratitude, injustice, misrepresentation, and lies, but we can be willing to let God take over: "God, You who could love the thief on the cross and the woman taken in adultery, You love these people, too."

What was required for the demonstration that I had to make? Was it not the ability to "nothingize" myself, even to the extent of not trying to be self-righteous about loving my enemy? When you say that you are loving your enemy, that is self-righteousness. We have to learn to let God do the loving and be willing to be an instrument through which God's love flows to our friends and to our enemies.

In the world there are good people and bad people, just and unjust people, but when you climb up into that circle of God you find that God is the principle of all people; God is the only principle of people, the animating love and life and truth of all people—those in your business, in your social relationships, and in your home.

Your home is a composite of your consciousness of home. You are the doorkeeper of your household and you should stand guard at the door to see that nothing gets past that door which does not have the right to be there. This door, however, is not a material door. The only door there is, is the door of consciousness, and the only door for which you are responsible is that door. What do you allow to get past your door, your consciousness? Do you accept contagion and infection as power in your home? Are you a party to discord and bickering? You should make it a matter of daily realization that nothing can enter the doorway of consciousness except the truth of being, and that no suggestion of human power, whether physical, material, or mental, is law. Any belief that enters your home must first enter through your consciousness, and the truth of being in your consciousness will act as a law of annihilation to any false belief that would intrude.

Everything that comes within range of your consciousness will take on the nature and character of that consciousness. Your own life is not only affected by what gets past the door of your consciousness, but the life of everyone who has brought himself to your consciousness is affected, and that includes the members of your family and sometimes the members of your community and church. All these look to you for bread; they look to you for the truth of being, but oftentimes your mind is so occupied with concern over your own discords and inharmonies that they are turned away without the divine substance which they sought from you.

Deep within every person is a hunger for the bread of life. Friends, relatives, and even acquaintances who find their way to your home ostensibly seeking companionship, supply, or any form of material good, even though from their point of view that may be their purpose, are in reality longing and craving for the true substance of life, the meat that perisheth not. If you give them money and give them that alone, if you give them your physical, human companionship, and give them that alone, you are giving them a stone: You are not giving them the bread of life; you are not lifting their state of consciousness. This you can do only in the degree that you are specifically entertaining the consciousness of truth within your being as they come to you:

God is the substance and the activity of my home; God is the consciousness of every individual who enters my home, whether it is family or friends. Nothing enters my home to contaminate or violate its sanctity, because God is my only home. As long as my home appears on earth as a material structure, it will express the harmony of God. Those in that home will either reflect that harmony or they will be removed because nothing unlike God can remain in my home—my temple, my being, my body. Anything of a discordant nature that would enter, or might temporarily be permitted to enter, will be removed in its time and in such a way that it will injure no one, but be a blessing to everyone involved.

Since God is my consciousness, nothing can enter that consciousness that "defileth or maketh a lie," and even if I, in my ignorance or human softness, permit something to enter which has no place there, it will not long remain. The consciousness of Truth and Life which I am will heal it or remove it. I am willing that everybody and everything that enters my consciousness shall be either healed or removed. I dare not cling to anyone and say, "With all your faults, I still need you and want you." I take my stand with God and, if necessary, leave father, mother, brother, sister, husband, or wife in order to dwell in the secret place of the most High.

Clinging to that which you know is not right just because of human emotion very often does much to impede your spiritual demonstration. Each one must rely upon inner guidance to determine when to let go of human ties and when not to let go.

Nearly every marriage ceremony contains some version of the statement, "that which God has joined together let no man put asunder." The truth is that what God has joined together, what God has brought together in oneness and unity, no man *can* put asunder. It would be an utter impossibility for man to have power over God and over God's work. No man has the power to undo the work of God. In the world of appearances, there can be temporary strife, discord and inharmony—and there will be, but not for you if you climb into that circle of God and there live in the constant realization that what God has made is forever, and what God has brought together no man can put asunder.

In dealing with a marital problem, you would realize that since God is one, the only relationship that exists is a relationship of oneness, and there can be no division or separation in that oneness—no inharmony or discord in one. The moment there are two, there can be any kind of discord and inharmony, but that is impossible in oneness.

Many people believe that a realization such as this would ensure a couple's remaining together, and that, therefore, no divorce or separation could possibly follow. Nothing could be further from the truth. A couple may be married and may be legally one, and yet they may not actually be one in their being—they may not be spiritually one. Therefore, this realization of oneness might bring about a separation or divorce much more quickly than would otherwise be the case, freeing both husband and wife from the yoke of inharmony and discord and enabling both to find their oneness elsewhere. No two people can realize oneness or true happiness when life resolves itself into a continuous battle of misunderstandings and disagreements. The marital relationship without love is a sin.

A practitioner of spiritual healing should never intrude into the family life of any person or of any couple, nor judge humanly as to whether two people should get married, remain married, be separated, or divorced. That is not the business of a spiritual healer, and, furthermore, there is no easy way of knowing from outward appearances what the truth of the situation is. In all cases of marital discord and inharmony, hold to the fact that God is the only one and there is only one marriage, the mystical marriage. Such a marriage is God-ordained, and no man can rend it asunder.

Sometimes the very best way that God can maintain that oneness is by severing the human or legal tie. Never believe for a minute that just knowing oneness will keep all marriages together, because it will not. Knowing oneness will keep a person one with his good; and if that good means celibacy, marriage, separation, or divorce, that is what will happen. No one has the right to outline how a demonstration is to take place because everything must unfold in accordance with spiritual good, not in accordance with some human being's idea of what constitutes good. No one should set himself up as being competent to decide what is humanly good.

It is unwise to attempt to protect loved ones from discords

and inharmonies which, knowingly or unknowingly, they have brought and are bringing upon themselves. It is better to give up anxious concern, loose them, and let them live with some of their discords, because the overprotection which would keep them from the results of their own conduct is often the stumbling block which prevents them from awakening to the truth of being. Their very suffering may be the needling necessary to awaken them. Each one of us has to learn the lesson of "loose him, and let him go." Loose your loved ones into Christ; loose them into God; and let the law of God govern.

Regardless of the amount of spiritual realization attained by some people and the measure of its practice in daily life, there are always those who for one reason or another cannot or will not respond. The greatest known witness to the spiritual life was the Master, Christ Jesus, and yet even he had his Judas, his doubting Thomas, his denying Peter, and his disciples who fell asleep in the Garden. Undoubtedly both Peter and Thomas awakened and atoned for their temporary lapse. Of Judas, there is no proof of any awakening to this spiritual light. Furthermore, there was a time when the spiritual impetus found no answer in Saul of Tarsus, and yet, at a certain given moment, he not only responded to it but he became a great living witness to it.

Therefore, no one need despair if those in his family, his church group, in his nation, or in the world at large are not responding at this moment to the spiritual impulse. In their own time they will. With some of them it may take days, weeks, months, years; and with some it may take many lifetimes to come. But sooner or later every knee will bend—every knee. At some time or other, all men will be taught of God.

People believe that they are held back because of the lack of demonstration of someone around them, or that for one reason or another the lack of demonstration on the part of someone else may have an adverse influence upon them. That could never be true unless they themselves permitted it. Each one is responsible for his own spiritual demonstration, and it is useless to blame the other fellow for a lack of spiritual courage.

No less an authority than the Master has taught that in order to attain the stature of Christhood, it is necessary to leave mother, father, brother, sister "for my sake." Why not face the fact that most people are not yet ready to leave those who they believe are acting in such a way as to hold back their demonstration? So no one should blame anyone—not even himself—but quickly realize that only the acceptance of a universal belief in a selfhood apart from God could hypnotize him into believing that any influence outside his own being could act upon him. How could anyone influence, help, or hinder another person's demonstration? How is it possible for anyone to come between him and his realization of Christhood? That can only be if there is a dependence on a human being.

If men and women accept the universal belief that their support and supply come from husband, wife, investments, or business, they have brought themselves under the law. Before people have any knowledge of spiritual wisdom, such a reliance is natural; but after they have learned the truth of their identity as being one with the Father, if they then persist in placing their "faith in princes"—their reliance on friends or family—instead of freeing themselves and living under grace, they will continue to live under the human law of limitation. In spiritual living there is no dependence upon any person or thing: There is a sharing, but there is never dependence. Whatever is shared with another is shared from the infinite bounty of God:

"I and my Father are one": That is my relationship to God, and that is God's relationship to me. It has nothing to do with any person: It has nothing to do with relatives, friends, or associates. My good is in no way dependent on

them, nor is their good dependent on me. My good is God's allness made manifest as my individual being.

When this oneness is glimpsed, every relationship becomes one of friendship, joy, and co-operation. If our dependence is not on others, then no lack or loss would be suffered if our relationships with others were wiped away because good is inherent in our relationship to God, and it does not lie within anyone's power to lose the relationship of joint-heir with Christ in God. The human picture does not testify to that because, in order to benefit by the relationship of Father and son, an activity of truth must take place in individual consciousness.

When you learn to "call no man on earth your father," automatically every man, woman, and child on this earth become your brother and sister. According to human testimony, you may be an only child and you may have no relatives on earth, but once you have agreed to "call no man on earth your father," that is no longer true because you have made a brother and sister of everybody in this universe. People who have looked upon you as a stranger suddenly feel, "I know this person; I feel as if I have always known him." Even though you are not blood-brothers or sisters no barrier exists between you, because now a higher relationship than that of blood-brother or sister has been established: Now you are brothers and sisters by divine ordinance.

There is a bond, a spiritual tie, which binds together all the children of God. This is not a tie to human beings or mortals, and that is why those who persist in remaining on the human or mortal level ultimately drift out of the experience of the more spiritually illumined. Each one draws unto himself those with whom he is spiritually united, his spiritual brothers and sisters; but those who live and insist on living on the mortal or material plane sooner or later drift away from him, and sometimes the greatest heartaches come from trying to hold on to them.

Along the way, you may meet with falsehood, deception, and villification; sometimes your friends and relatives are asleep, not upholding you, sometimes even resisting or obstructing you. You must reach the point in your unfoldment where that is of no consequence to you. It makes no difference in your life who fails you: It makes a difference only to them because they have failed in their demonstration of their Christhood, but it will make no difference to you if you have learned your relationship to God.

Since God is the life, wisdom, activity, and supply of your being, you have no demonstration to make which is dependent upon anyone here on earth. You are spiritually fed, clothed, and housed. Your utter and complete reliance is on this truth that all that the Father has is yours. If the whole earth were wiped away, this one truth would remain, "I and my Father are one," and all that the Father has would still be yours.

When the Master taught his disciples to leave mother, brother, sister for his sake, he did not mean that they should leave those of their spiritual household. "Who is my mother, or my brethren? And he looked round about on them which sat about him, and said, Behold my mother and my brethren! For whosoever shall do the will of God, the same is my brother, and my sister, and mother." All who can meet together on a spiritual level of love are bound together from now until eternity, sharing forever with each other.

CHAPTER XII

GOD IS OUR DESTINY

Spirit is forever in operation drawing unto us our own, whatever that own is, whether in human relationships or in business. There is an invisible activity which draws us to our rightful employment, our rightful marriage, our rightful city, or our rightful nation. Day by day the Father gives us the work of each day, and with that work always comes the recompense and reward.

Most of us would perhaps agree that the majority of the problems besetting us have to do with regrets for the past or fears of the future. Usually at the present moment we are all right. If we could live in this minute, content to know that the power of God is in operation and be willing to let that continue, there would be no concern about the past and very little about the future. In one way or another, we would know day by day what to do, and sometimes we might even know a few weeks in advance. It has been my experience that God seldom reveals what His purpose is for me very far in advance.

When you reach the stage in your experience where your life is a devotion to whatever of a constructive nature you are doing at the moment and you recognize that your livelihood is coincidental to that work; when you can find something in your work that is in the nature of a service to be performed, never again will your business be a burden and never will it be a failure.

Living from day to day with the one objective of making money or making a living may result in success, but on the other hand it may just as possibly result in failure. The ultimate outcome is not foreordained. But when you have found something into which you can put your heart and soul, into which you can pour out some measure of service, even if in the beginning it is the most menial of labors, if you can find that the doing of your work is of some service to somebody, it will lead you on to higher forms of activity.

If your consciousness is filled with service and co-operation, then your activity, regardless of its nature, will express the service and co-operation in your consciousness, and it will be a steadily expanding and unfolding activity.

The Infinity which is God constitutes the infinity of my being. It is not that I of my own self am infinite; it is because there is only one Infinity, and that is God; and since God is my individual being, my individual being embraces infinity. In that infinity, all is included: Nothing can be added to me and nothing can be taken from me.

What could hinder you from experiencing that Infinity? Only the attempt to get something, to desire something, or to believe that you have earned or are deserving of something.

Close your eyes, fill yourself full of God, and then be a beholder and see what miraculous things God does through you, although not always according to your expectation or not always at the time that you think they should be done. There is a spiritual demonstration for every child of God, and you are that child of God "if so be that the Spirit of God dwell in you."

When a person seeks to reach a predetermined goal, such as an opportunity to go into some particular business or to change from one position to another, he holds himself on the wheel of human existence, rather than opening himself to live by divine grace. It may be that divine grace will provide a way so that he will not be in bondage to any established pattern of life, but be lifted into some new and heretofore unthought of activity.

To desire any *thing* or any *person* is to remain on the wheel of human existence. What you really should want, and all you can legitimately try to demonstrate, is a greater awareness of the Christ. If you had the realization of God's presence, you would have infinite good; but when you seek a demonstration of something other than the presence of God, you are merely trying to demonstrate limitation, and you will succeed in doing just that. If, however, you are living these principles of The Infinite Way, you will realize the infinite nature of life. Then you are not under the law; you are under grace, a way of life without limit.

The first time I ever gave a talk to a group in a metaphysical center, a woman came up to me with a list of nine things she wanted and asked me to pray that she get them. When I quickly returned the list to her with an, "I'm sorry. Not only would I not pray for these things for you, but I do not even care particularly if you ever get them," she was very much surprised because she thought that was what truth was for: She thought God was to be used.

The purpose of demonstration is the demonstration of the Christ-consciousness which is divine grace and which nullifies all karmic law. It is a karmic law that man is condemned to earn his living by the sweat of his brow as a punishment for past deeds. Certainly as long as he works for the sole purpose of earning a livelihood, he is under karmic law. If you are beginning to glimpse what I am trying to say and if you want to be released from the wheel of life and stop working for the purpose of making a living, you do not give up your job: You first break the karmic law, and then you will find that you will no longer have to work for a livelihood.

When I make such a statement, people often retort, "How can you say that, when you, yourself, continue to work for a living?" I can only assure them that that is not true, and furthermore, it has not been true since 1928. I do not work for a living: I work for the joy of the work. Does anybody work twenty hours a day as I do just for a living? No, I do this work because it is given to me by divine grace, and the livelihood is the natural result.

Let no reader misunderstand this. I am not saying that you do not have to work. I am saying that you do not have to work *for a living*. There is a vast difference. The closer you come to living by grace, the more you will work and the harder you will work. Only then, it will not be for a living; it will be for the joy of expressing yourself, and the living will be wholly incidental to that expression. As a matter of fact, your livelihood may come from some other source which may entirely save you the necessity of working and thereby free you for some other activity. But whatever its apparent source, it will be from the one Source.

Everyone in the human picture is under karmic law, under the law of "whatsoever a man soweth, that shall he also reap," but anyone can break that law through the realization that he does not live by bread alone: He lives by grace, by every word of God.

If you were called upon for help in a case of unemployment, your treatment would probably consist of the realization that God, being infinite and the only being, must be both employer and employee. In other words, God is the only one; and inasmuch as there are not two, there cannot be one to employ and one to be employed. There is only oneness, oneness of being, and God is the only being: God is infinitely and eternally employed; God is about His own business, and the son of God must always be employed and about the Father's business.

"In all thy ways acknowledge him, and he shall direct thy paths." This may be simple to do when the favors and all the good things of life are being showered upon you; but when they are seemingly withheld, are you as able or as quick to say, "Thank You, Father, that too must be a part of Your activity"? You must acknowledge God in all your ways, not

in some of them. Humanly, there are times when there seem
to be failures. Even for these, thank God because, through
your recognition of God, failure too may result in a higher
good. Failure may prove a blessing if you have the vision
to turn to the next thing instead of staying in the rut where
you have remained due to some temporary success. Acknowledge Him in all your ways—whether it seems to be failure
or success.

Give up now once and for all the belief that you can succeed or that you can fail. *You* will never succeed, but *you*
will never fail: *You* will forever and forever show forth God's
handiwork; you will forever be that place in consciousness
where God shines through. The glory of your being is not the
glory of *your* being: It is the glory of God's being. Do you
see why the great masters of all time have revealed that
humility is the beginning of wisdom, but that humility is not
self-depreciation? No, humility is the realization of God's
allness. It is not depreciating yourself, but on the contrary,
it is understanding yourself as that which shows forth the full
and complete glory of God. The light of God is your light;
the wisdom of God is your wisdom; the love of God is your
love.

*Thank You, thank You, Father, I am the instrument of
Your being. I have no wisdom of my own; I have no age, no
body, no Soul of my own; I have no goodness of my own.
There is but one good, but one life—the Father in heaven—
and I am that place where the fullness of the glory of the
Godhead shines through.*

It is not your understanding or ability that will ever help
you or anyone else: It is God's understanding and ability of
which you permit yourself to be the avenue, just as a composer permits melodies to flow through him. Is the composer
the creator of the music? Is the poet the creator of poetry?
Is the artist the creator of the sculpture or painting? No, every
creative artist is but the avenue through which the creative

capacity of God expresses. He is the instrument, the paint-brush, the chisel and the hammer in the hands of God. That is all a poet is; that is all a painter or sculptor is; that is all you and I are.

We are the instruments in the hands of God. We are the vehicles, or the tools, used by the Father to show forth His handiwork and His glory. The healthier and happier and the more prosperous we are, the greater witnesses we are. To what? To our understanding? No, to God's grace flowing through us. God's grace! That is really the source of every-thing. We are the recipients, the witnesses to God's grace, and we share it with each other. It does not belong to me and it does not belong to you. It is of the Father—divine grace flowing through us.

If we always sought spiritual guidance in every activity of our experience with no attempt to translate it into the human realm, we would be so spiritually fulfilled and illumined, that that illumination would lead us not only to our true spiritual teaching, but even to such mundane things as finding the right dress, the right car, or the right apartment. In the scale of God, there is no difference in these things.

God is fulfillment. Spiritual illumination cannot come to you without bringing with it your correct employment or your rightful home. God cannot be divided; God is not divisible: The activity of God does not include one thing and leave out another. God could not reveal Itself to you as some form of right activity and then leave you without supply, and God could not reveal Itself as supply and leave out right activity.

Often it seems that these do not appear simultaneously, but this is because you have prayed amiss. You have prayed a divided prayer: You are praying for *things* or praying that Spirit reveal Itself only in certain directions instead of praying that God reveal Itself as light, as the fullness of light, the full-ness of illumination, the fullness of truth. God's garment is whole, complete, and perfect. When God places the mantle about your shoulders, it includes your entire being.

Do not go to God and expect a healing; do not go to God and expect employment; do not go to God and expect safety or security: Go to God expecting God. Go to God expecting to receive the spiritual awareness of His presence. Watch how It then appears outwardly as the harmonies of your daily experience in simple little things like finding a parking place, or finding a seat ready on an airplane, or a room in a hotel when it is crowded.

In simple things or in the very deepest experiences of your life, you will find completeness and perfection by seeking the Father in Spirit and as Spirit. Do not seek to divide the garment. Do not pray for health or wealth, safety or security, or peace on earth. Pray only that God reveal Itself as truth. Pray for light, for truth, for more wisdom, for illumination. Seek the whole garment: Seek truth, light, revelation, illumination. Worship Him as Spirit and let the whole garment descend upon you and reveal Itself as supply, as home, as joyous relationship, as right activity.

CHAPTER XIII

A NEW CONCEPT OF SUPPLY

Supply is one of the easiest demonstrations that a spiritual student can make, but there is a vast difference between the spiritual truth about supply and the human sense of it. In spiritual truth, supply is not income; it is outgo. To human sense, the reverse of that is true. Spiritually, however, there is no way to demonstrate supply. It cannot be done because all the supply that exists in heaven or on earth exists within you at this moment, and, therefore, all attempts to demonstrate supply must result in failure. There is no supply outside of your being. If you want to enjoy the abundance of supply, you must open out a way for that supply to escape. How you can loose this supply by giving will be revealed to you in your communion with God.

When someone calls upon you for help in gaining a consciousness of supply and seeks instruction, it is legitimate and necessary to call his attention to the principle of supply in some such fashion as this, "Certainly, I will give you help, but you can begin to gain this consciousness of supply by trying to find something you can give some place where you have not been giving—not to your family, because you are probably doing that already, but to someone who is not a member of your family or even to someone who at the moment is your enemy. Search your clothes closet or your pantry to see if there is not something there that you can spare. Start the flow of giving, and you will start the flow of supply."

Your knowing the truth of the infinite and omnipresent nature of supply will set your patient free from the belief of lack and limitation; and as he begins to release the forms of supply and develops an attitude of giving rather than of getting, the supply will begin to flow. There is no limit to what a spiritual student can begin to give away. This "giving away" has no relationship to amounts—to the number of dollars or of anything else: Giving has to do with the degree of *givingness*. It is the acknowledgment that supply is giving out, not gathering in.

Giving need not necessarily begin with the giving of anything material, money or things—with *giving* anything. It may begin with the giving *up* of some things: the giving up of resentment, jealousy, and hate; the giving up of the desire to get recognition, reward, remuneration, gratitude, and co-operation. Simultaneously with this "giving up" will come the *giving* of patience, co-operation, love, and forgiveness. Give in the realization that it is not what you get that is your supply: It is what you give.

It may be that you have been holding on too tightly to money. If so you will have to learn how to release it, and by turning it loose, set in motion the flow that inevitably returns to you. This is not to be construed as throwing money or any good thing away prodigally or carelessly. No one is ever called upon for more than meets with common sense or more than wisdom dictates. What is called for is a change in attitude and a willingness to begin at any particular moment to give with the idea that there is this quarter or this dollar to send out into circulation, and the important thing is that it begins to circulate.

This is not a new idea. Scripture has given us this teaching under the name of tithing, that is, the giving of one tenth of one's income to God. There are many people who believe that they cannot afford to give such an amount because in their hearts they believe that that would be too much of a drain on their pocketbooks, and it may be that for them to try to do this might be disastrous at first. It might be wiser for those people to begin tithing a smaller amount—5 per cent, 4 per cent, 3 per cent, 2 per cent, or any amount—as long as a specific sum or percentage is set aside which has a priority over all other expenditures and which is given to some *impersonal* purpose, not to family, not for one's own benefit, but to something completely impersonal.

Probably the majority of people believe that the gift of a tithe should be taken from what is left over after all other expenses have been met. The secret of tithing, however, is not to give the residue, but to give the "first fruits" to God and, furthermore, to give these first fruits secretly wherever possible so that only the giver knows whence it comes.

After learning how easy it is to give 2 or 3 per cent of one's income, in a short time the amount may be increased to 4 or 5 per cent and then to 10 per cent. Interestingly enough, rarely does tithing stop at 10 per cent. I have known three different people who tithed 80 per cent of all their income, and, surprising as it may seem, these people had more left to live on, and with, than they could possibly spend even if they were very extravagant.

Let me repeat this important aspect of the principle of supply: Supply is not getting; supply is giving. The bread that you cast upon the water is the bread that comes back to you. It is not your neighbor's bread; it is your own bread; and if you have not cast it upon the water, there will be no bread to come back to you. All the bread on the water is earmarked for return to the person who has sent it forth.

In one way or another you must cast bread upon the waters. If you have not learned how to do this, this is your first great lesson. Because of the infinite nature of your being, you cannot add health to yourself or wealth or opportunity or companionship: All you can do is to recognize that you embody all that God is and has. You must not try to get; you must not try to have; you must not try to draw to you: You must learn how to let Infinity flow out from you. The coming

back of the bread is a reflex action that takes place of its
own accord, like throwing a rubber ball against a wall. You
throw it, but it bounces back of its own accord.

As you cast your bread upon the waters, you will find the
grace of God flowing into expression as the harmony of your
being. If you ignore this important point in spiritual teaching
or if you think that after all it is not too important, you may
very possibly miss the way, because the longer you hold
yourself in bondage to the belief that you can get something
—even from God—just that long are you separating yourself
from contact with your good. The moment you can realize
the instantaneity of now and the *I*-ness of being, from that
moment you look out on this world in the joyous recognition:

Thank You, Father, I have no desires: I need nothing but
Thy grace; I need no one but Thee. Let me live every single
minute as I am living this minute, loving this universe and
loving everyone in it. I hold nothing against any man: No
one can come within range of my consciousness who needs
forgiving because I have already forgiven him—seventy times
seven.

A second, and equally important, part of the principle of
supply is that supply is invisible. You cannot see, hear, touch,
taste, or smell supply; you have never seen supply because
supply does not exist in the visible realm. Supply is Spirit,
or Life, completely invisible and infinite in nature.

There is today no less supply than Jesus had, than Moses,
Elisha, or Elijah had. They knew that they had an infinity
and they proved it. You have exactly that same infinity, not
one farthing less. But until it becomes clear to you that
God constitutes individual being, you cannot understand
the infinite nature of your own being, and you will always
be seeking supply and security outside of yourself, security in
dollar bills or even in bills of a much larger denomination.

The belief that money and property constitute supply
has been accepted for so many years that most people rely

on them for their security; and then when, through the devaluation of the currency or through a world-wide depression or for some other reason beyond their control, billions disappear, they feel that their world has collapsed. Students of spiritual wisdom must come to the realization that they have no supply outside their own being, that supply lies in something that cannot be known through the physical senses: Supply is the Infinite Invisible.

Supply is something within your own being: It is the truth that God constitutes your being. When you recognize God as your being, you will have no need other than to know Him aright. If you have God, you have supply; but the important point is, do you have God? Spiritually, yes, theoretically, yes, everyone has God; but if everyone had God, there would be no lack or limitation in all this world. Actually people merely have God as a potentiality or a possibility. Having God means consciously to know Him aright, consciously to tabernacle with Him, consciously to commune with Him, consciously to know Him as the very *I* of your being. Having that, you have the source of all supply.

Moses had God, and that is why Moses could witness manna falling from the sky when he needed it; Elijah had God, and that is why Elijah, out in the wilderness, could be fed by ravens or could wake up one morning and find cakes being baked right on the stones in front of him. Out of what? Out of nothing—out of nothing visible or tangible. These things came to them out of their consciousness of God appearing as the substance and form of life, God appearing as food. Having God, they had all.

The world is losing itself in such statements as "God will take care of this," "God will do this," or "God will do that"—and God does not do it at all. It is only in proportion to the God-experience that it is done. Everyone must eventually come to the realization that having God, he has all; and not having God, regardless of what else he has, he has nothing. Nothing is withheld, nothing is missing, and nothing is absent from the person who has achieved God-awareness.

"Yes, yes," you may say to yourself as you read this, "yes, all this sounds good on paper, but how can I arrive at the consciousness of that supply which is continuously eluding me?"

Let us go back again to our original premise. Since God is infinite, there exists nothing but God. Then there is no supply other than God. When you perceive the infinity of God and that God in Its infinity is closer to you than breathing, you can then begin to claim for yourself an infinite abundance. In making such a claim, you will not be insulting your intelligence because what you are now claiming is the presence of God in you, the presence of infinite, omnipresent God.

It is not easy for anyone to drop completely from his mind all concern as to where his next automobile is coming from, his next vacation trip, or in some cases even his next meal; it is not easy to put into practice the Master's teaching to "take no thought for your life, what ye shall eat, or what ye shall drink; nor yet for your body, what ye shall put on"; but nevertheless one of the most important steps in developing a consciousness of supply is to drop these concerns from your mind because the forms of good are but the added things. In other words, your outward good is but the symbol of the omnipresence of supply.

If you do not have a consciousness of supply, you will not have the symbols of supply in your pocket. First, there must be the consciousness of supply, and then the symbols follow. When you have the consciousness of the presence of God wherever you are, when you have the realization that the place whereon you stand is holy ground and that "Son, thou art ever with me, and all that I have is thine"—when you have that consciousness, the symbols appear as they are needed. The symbols vary from day to day: They take the form of money one day, transportation or hotel accommodations the next day, food, clothing, or some other good the following day. Whatever it may be, it appears as needed since it is but the symbol or outer expression of supply.

Again let me repeat: Supply itself can never be cognized through the senses. Supply is God; supply is Spirit; supply is the presence of the Lord with you; supply is a Life-force that works through you.

What further proof does the spiritually receptive person need of the truth of this than to visualize a fruit tree in the off-season when there is no fruit and when there are not even blossoms on the tree? Because the tree is barren are you going to cut it down? Why not? There is no supply there—no visible supply. To all appearances the tree is barren. Ah, but you know better than that. You know that there is a Life-force operating in and through that tree, a Life-force that is forming the sap which will go up through the trunk, out into the branches, and which will later appear as the blossoms, and then later as the fruit. You are not misled by the appearance of a barren tree into believing that the tree has no supply of fruit or that the tree is useless.

Why not apply this same principle to your own life and affairs and trust it regardless of the state of your visible supply at any given moment? If a hurricane should come and blow your whole world away, you would still be standing on holy ground, that earth which is "the Lord's, and the fullness thereof," because I am there, and that invisible, infinite, and all-loving Life-force would still be operating in your consciousness. With a little patience, the blossoms and the fruit will appear again in the form of dollar bills or whatever the need may be. All that is necessary is the recognition of this truth.

Believe this or not as you choose: There is a Life-force operating in you, just as it is operating in the tree. But you ask, "Why has it not become visible in greater measure? Why must I struggle endlessly with this problem of lack?"

Can it be because your consciousness is not attuned to the Invisible, but only to the visible? Can it be that most of the time you have been trying and still are trying to create supply from the visible? Loaves and fishes cannot be multiplied from anything in the visible, nor can dollar bills. If anyone attempted to multiply dollar bills, he would very quickly find himself in jail. Therefore, if anyone wants more dollar bills, he must do his multiplying in the Invisible. And the manner of it? Realize that God is infinite and that your supply is as infinite as God.

And what about those who let their fruit stay on the tree, who do not pluck it? How quickly they learn that a tree can wither and give forth no more fruit: Only as you pluck the fruit and gather the blossoms from the flower bushes does the Life-force begin its work of multiplication, pushing out twice as much as before.

Your supply becomes evident only in the proportion that you love your neighbor—give out love, give out forgiveness, give out co-operation—but *give always without seeking a return*. Only the gross materialist gives and then seeks a return. The true spiritual light gives out of the fullness of a heart of givingness, seeking no return. There is no need for any kind of a return: God is one's sufficient return.

To understand this is to understand one of the major healing principles of The Infinite Way: Your consciousness of truth determines your supply, not a God somewhere, not a Christ somewhere, not a Spirit somewhere; but your consciousness—*your developed state of consciousness*. Very few in all the world are born with a consciousness of truth full-blown. Nearly always it is a matter of developing that consciousness. The consciousness of the fishermen-disciples was a *developed* state of consciousness. The consciousness of Saul of Tarsus developed into the consciousness of St. Paul. St. Augustine in early life was far from being a spiritual light, but he also became a *developed* state of spiritual consciousness.

The secret is that the source of your supply is your own consciousness of God as supply—your *developed* state of consciousness. If you seek supply through the help of a practitioner, then your supply is dependent on the developed spiritual consciousness of your practitioner. But that will not be a permanent demonstration of supply because sooner or later you will be placed in a position where you will have to rely on your own developed state of consciousness, always remembering that that developed consciousness is God-consciousness unfolding as your individual consciousness.

It is then that you begin to drop in a measure the personal sense of supply and arrive at a great and grand moment in your life when the whole world falls off your shoulders, when you say and believe with all your heart:

"The earth is the Lord's, and the fullness thereof . . . Son, all that I have is thine." The fullness of God's glory—not just a part of it, but the fullness—is now mine, swallowing up mortality with its limited sense of life and clothing me with immortality, swallowing up my finite sense of self that I may be clothed upon with God's infinity, God's grace, God's presence, and God's power.

I have no power of my own; I of my own self can do nothing; I of my own self am nothing. If I speak of myself and my power and my supply, I bear witness to a lie. The Father is my life; the Father is my supply.

I am invisible; my supply is invisible, and I carry it with me wherever I go.

Some spiritual seekers mistakenly entertain the fantastic idea that, in some mysterious manner, God is much better to them than to the rest of the world. What a horrible God that would be! True, an ignorance of truth may bring your neighbor face to face with insufficiency and leave him under a claim of lack or limitation, but God does not bestow His bounties more freely upon one than upon another. The only difference is that some, and particularly some on the Path, are more consciously aware of God's presence manifest as form.

No seeker dare believe that one nation, one race, or one religion has more access to God than another, or that any one person has some special status with God. The infinity of God is universal, but it is your apprehension of that truth that constitutes your demonstration of good. When you comprehend that a realization of God's presence results in the actual manifestation and expression of abundance, you will not believe that through some miraculous treatment or prayer anything has been increased: You will understand that what has happened is that you have become more aware of that which already existed from the beginning in its fullness.

In the very city where one person experiences lack and limitation, another is enjoying abundance. The city is not responsible, nor is the time responsible. It may be a year of depression or one of prosperity. The year is not responsible; many people have lost all their possessions in boom years. The place cannot make you and the place cannot break you; the time cannot make you and the time cannot break you. You, yourself, become a law to your experience in proportion as you realize God to be the substance of all form.

If God is the substance of all form, can you increase the amount of the form? Is God the substance of limited form? No, the form is already infinite, as infinite as the substance of which it is made. The secret lies in the acknowledgment of God as omnipresent—more than that, as Omnipresence Itself, the presence of your very being, and therefore the presence of Infinity. Your awareness of the presence of Infinity reveals Infinity where the lack has been.

Everything that appears is made out of the substance of the Invisible, and it is infinite. For example, there is no way to increase your supply of crops, money, land, or of anything else by what the world calls prayer. There is no miracle of prayer that produces rabbits out of hats. Nobody can do that unless the rabbits were there in the first place.

There is no such thing as increase or decrease: There is only Infinity expressing Itself. If you are not the recipient of the bounty of Infinity, it is not because Infinity is absent: It is because of your lack of awareness of Infinity.

Too many metaphysicians are trying to demonstrate *forms* of good, while all the time there is no form of good separate and apart from Good, Itself. In proportion as the consciousness of God is demonstrated, that presence of Good appears in the form necessary to your experience of the moment, sometimes in the most miraculous ways.

Throughout the Bible, from Genesis to Revelation, this miracle is told and retold. Every prophet, saint, seer, or sage has had an awareness of God's presence, has lived consciously in that Presence, and has found his protection, food, safety, and security appearing as whatever was his need. But was everybody in biblical times thus cared for? Is everybody today thus cared for? You know the answer. Then to whom did it happen, to whom does it happen, and to whom will it happen? To the person consciously aware of God's presence, the person living, moving, and having his being consciously in God. The Master could not multiply loaves and fishes: The Master had only one realization —the presence of the Father within—and His consciousness of the presence of the Father within appeared outwardly as the multiplication of fishes, as healings, and as the raising of the dead.

As you learn to give up using mental power—striving to accomplish something with truth, or attempting to make a powerhouse out of the human mind—and become still and receptive until the Word begins to flow, you will know the meaning of harmony and of infinity.

Watch the miracle as your mind gives up the struggle to create, to increase, to heal, to save, or to redeem. Watch the miracle that takes place in your life as you learn to relax in the realization that the infinite nature of God makes God the only *Is*, and that even the *forms* as which God ᴊppears must be infinite. So the heavens declare the glory of God by showing forth the infinite beauty and bounty of God; the earth shows forth the handiwork of God, the glory of God in infinite form, variety, color, perfume, and amount.

Infinity is the measure of God. The moment, however, that you try to demonstrate apples, you have descended to finiteness; the minute you try to demonstrate a home, health, or wealth, you are in finiteness. But, if you demonstrate the realization of God's presence, you have God's presence appearing as infinity in infinite forms of good. The presence of God does not manufacture some form of harmony: The presence of God is Itself the form of all good.

CHAPTER XIV

UNDER THE SHADOW OF THE ALMIGHTY

Then shalt thou walk in thy way safely, and thy foot shall not stumble. PROVERBS 3:23

Be strong and courageous, be not afraid nor dismayed for the king of Assyria, nor for all the multitude that is with him: for there be more with us than with him:

With him is an arm of flesh; but with us in the Lord our God to help us, and to fight our battles. II CHRONICLES 32:7, 8

The God of my rock; in him will I trust: he is my shield, and the horn of my salvation, my high tower, and my refuge, my saviour; thou savest me from violence. II SAMUEL 22:3

The Lord is my rock, and my fortress, and my deliverer; my God, my strength, in whom I will trust; my buckler, and the horn of my salvation, and my high tower. PSALM 18:2

As the mountains are round about Jerusalem, so the Lord is round about his people from henceforth even for ever.
PSALM 125:2

For I, saith the Lord, will be unto her a wall of fire round about, and will be the glory in the midst of her.
ZECHARIAH 2:5

The Bible is filled with promises of safety to those who live consciously in the presence of God. It testifies to a God who is available in every experience and in every circum

154

stance of our existence; but it does not promise the world immunity from disaster—from earthquake, floods, or fire. As long as human beings are living in this world, they will experience some of the cataclysmic effects of the world's materialistic thinking. But the promise is clear that if there is famine, if there are floods, if there is fire, war, or bombs, those who live in God will walk *through* them, they will not in any wise touch them. Why is this? Why should they be singled out to be saved from the world's disasters?

Most churchgoing people assume that these biblical promises of safety apply to them, that they are of the household of God and are the ones to whom these evils will not come nigh. But strangely enough when war and disaster come, these very persons who have led good and upright lives are no more saved than anyone else, and it is for that reason that the world today is so seriously divided as to whether or not the promises of God are really true. One of the causes of the skepticism and the gross materialism in the world is that so few people, even church people, have found themselves exempt from the disasters of the world despite the fact that they have been members of churches since birth and have attended Sunday services and sometimes even mid-week services.

How can anyone know whether or not he is to be among those who will not suffer the disasters of the world? Everyone would like to escape, but the degree of immunity is determined by each person for himself. There is no God determining that for him. There is no power setting some apart to be saved while all the others are destroyed. Only by an understanding of, and obedience to, the laws of God as set forth in Scripture is he saved.

Scripture contains the laws of successful living, safe and secure living, and in the 91st Psalm is found the quintessence of these rules:

He that dwelleth in the secret place of the most High shall abide under the shadow of the Almighty.

Are we dwelling in the secret place of the most High? Do we live and move and have our being in God-consciousness? Do we live and move and have our being in a complete and utter reliance on the presence and power of God? Do we live and move and have our consciousness in an attitude of love, of giving and sharing? Do we live as if we really believed that the place whereon we stand is holy ground, that right here and now the presence and power of God envelops me and mine? Do we live from early morning until late at night in the conviction that God is directing our path? Do we live and move and have our being in the attitude of listening for God's direction, for God's guidance and protection? Are we living and moving and having our being in the realization that underneath are the everlasting arms? If we are, we are of the elect, of the household of God; we are of that heritage whose gift is righteousness and peace on earth.

"Thou wilt keep him in perfect peace, whose mind is stayed on thee." Are we of those who keep our mind stayed on God in reliance, confidence, hope, and expectancy? Or have we divided our allegiance between a faith in God and an equal, if not greater, faith in some human ruler, potentate, or power? Are we of those who acknowledge that God is our life, and, therefore, our life is indestructible, invincible, immortal, eternal, harmonious, vital, useful? Are we continuously acknowledging God in all our ways, acknowledging that God is our mind and, therefore, only infinite Intelligence can express Itself as the activity of our being? Or do we sometimes lean on our human understanding? Are we acknowledging God as the one infinite power, understanding that that terrifying human power, whether it appears as armies in the field or cancer of the body, is but the "arm of flesh," and therefore it is without power and jurisdiction in our experience? Are we acknowledging God as the main theme of our life, the source of our supply, the activity of our being?

Do we acknowledge God upon waking in the morning? Do

we acknowledge that only the power of God could have given us rest or sleep and that only the power and presence of God could awaken us to a new day?

Here, in this new day, God is the governor: God is the Lord and Master of this day, and God—not my bank account, not my job, not my family, not my friends, but God—controls the issues of the day. God governs and rules the day. God is the power that never slumbers and never sleeps. God is omnipresent with me throughout my slumbers and my rest. God is resting me even if I cannot sleep.

The acknowledgment of God as the real essence of our being, the real law of our being, the protection and supply of our being, is the acknowledgment of Him in all our ways.

In the human picture, there are many times when we are faced with situations that seem humanly impossible to meet or to be met. Everyone has that experience some time or other. Jesus had it in the garden of Gethsemane, on the road to Golgotha, and on the Cross.

Moses faced apparently insurmountable obstacles in leading the Hebrews out of bondage when Pharaoh's armies were so close behind them that it seemed inevitable that they would be captured and destroyed or else returned to bondage. But it was in those experiences that that which could not humanly be managed, spiritually appeared—the cloud by day, the pillar of fire by night, the manna from the sky, the water from the rocks. Moses probably never dreamed of such a form of protection. He probably never prayed for a cloud by day or a pillar of fire by night. His prayer was a realization of God's presence, but because God's presence was needed as protection, it came forth as a cloud by day and a pillar of fire by night. What happened the next day? The Red Sea opened. Do you for a moment believe that Moses could have prayed or even have thought of opening the Red Sea? No, no more than could you or I. His consciousness of God's presence appeared as the Red Sea opening.

In feeding and healing the multitudes and in his ability to disappear through the throngs when there was no human help available, the Master relied upon Something much greater than any human aid: He drew upon the Infinite Invisible for his every need. Let us not forget, however, that spiritual help always came through the spiritually enlightened leaders and not through the people themselves. Only the spiritually enlightened could be the avenues through which the miracles of God could take place.

Today, with the exception of enlightened clergymen, practitioners, and teachers who are willing to undertake some measure of individual healing for us, there are no spiritual leaders to do our work for us. Each one of us must come to the realization that God is no respecter of persons and that spiritual power is achieved in proportion to the devotion to that purpose. It is still true as it was in biblical times: "Thou wilt keep him in perfect peace, whose mind is stayed on thee." That is the one requisite—not whether we are highborn or lowborn, not whether we have great education or no education, not whether we are white, black, or yellow. It is determined by the activity of our own consciousness:

The word of God is quick and sharp and powerful; and in that Word, I have a protection within me greater than anything that is in the external realm. I have meat that ye know not of; I have food and drink and medicine and wine; I have inspiration, life, truth, and love. Within me is the word of God, and It is greater than anything that is in the world.

The word of God is quick and sharp and powerful, but the Word must be entertained by us in our individual consciousness; it must be in our hearts and on our lips. It must abide with us. "If ye abide in me"—if you let *Me* abide in you! Do you remember that the Master said that the whole world would disappear and disintegrate, but not "my word"?

No, the word of Truth will never fail or disappear because it has found lodgment in the consciousness of an individual here and there. If the entire world were destroyed, there would be a remnant left, and that remnant would consist of those who had the Word in their hearts. It is that remnant with the Word in their hearts which would begin the new race, the new generation, the new age. As we learn to abide in the Word and let that Word abide in us, we shall find that we are divinely led, divinely supported, divinely maintained, and divinely sustained.

In his much-quoted poem, "Invictus," William Ernest Henley confidently asserts:

> I am the master of my fate;
> I am the captain of my soul.

Certainly, in the spiritual sense, it is our responsibility to be the captain of our ship and the master of our soul, not by any kind of a hocus-pocus power, but in the degree that we can realize God as the only presence and only power. In the degree of that realization, are we led to be in the right place at the right time rather than in the wrong place at the wrong time.

When we live the ordinary human life and humanly decide to go across the ocean, we go. If the ship arrives safely, well and good, and if not we may be involved in an accident. However, if we are living this life of conscious God-realization morning, noon, and night, realizing God as our very mind, and realizing that God makes every decision, not we, there would be a guidance and protection which would keep us from injury.

As human beings living a human life, we are subject to all the beliefs that are floating about in the universe—the belief of chance, change, luck, astrology, circumstances, and whims of fate—but if we are dwelling in the Word, we are a law, not only unto our own experience, but we become the law unto all those who look to us for help in proportion as our consciousness is imbued or activated with Truth.

Practically every news report emphasizes that we are living through days of fear such as have never been known heretofore, and as far as the world is concerned, to date no defense has been found, no bombproof shelter invented which is secure against nuclear bombs—atomic or hydrogen. Therefore it is easy to be hypnotized by this fear into believing that our life is dependent upon the good nature or whim of our enemy. What a horrifying thought, and the more horrifying because it is not true!

We do not need to fear; we need have no part in the world's fears. Scripture reminds us that God is a fortress. Shall we take issue with the Bible? Shall we state that God is not our fortress in whom we place reliance? Is it not true that God is a high tower; is it not true that we live and move and have our being in God? Do we need God and cement, too? Have not some of us proved over and over again that we do not need God and medicine, and have not many proved that they do not need God and stone fortresses? God is our fortress, but that must be taken literally. God is a Spirit; God is infinite; and our life is hid with Christ in God.

Unless these truths are practiced, however, the Bible is nothing more nor less than a book on a table; it is not the living demonstrable Word. Actually, it is true that we live in God and God in us, "I am in the Father, and the Father in me"; but just as we have discovered that supply and health are invisible, so we must recognize that safety and security are invisible properties of God. We must dwell in the secret place of the most High, not go there exclusively on Sunday, but make it our constant habitation, morning, noon, and night; and this we do if we can realize that we ourselves are invisible. In fact, the whole secret of spiritual living has to do with the Invisible; it has to do with our recognition of the fact that our life is invisible, our life is hid with Christ in God.

The Master taught that if this temple, this visible form,

were destroyed, "in three days I will raise it up." Nothing can touch the *I*. Bullets cannot destroy It; flames cannot burn It; water cannot drown It—nothing can touch It because Life is invisible, and that means your life and my life: Our life is invisible, hid with Christ in God.

That very invisibility is our assurance of safety and security whether in the home or office, whether traveling by plane, automobile, or boat. We are invisible Infinity, God made flesh, infinite individual Consciousness, the consciousness of God in which everything is embodied and which includes within Itself even every mode of transportation.

Can there be any fear, then, of sinking ships, falling airplanes, or crashing automobiles? We are never "in" a ship, "on" an airplane, or "in" an automobile: The ship, the airplane, or the automobile is "in" us—in our consciousness. Every vehicle we encounter on the highway is in our consciousness; therefore, we need have no fear of poor drivers or drunken drivers on the road as long as we maintain an awareness of our consciousness as one with God. We are not victims of a driver outside of ourselves; every driver we encounter is within our consciousness and subject to our consciousness of truth. Every person who is at the controls of any vehicle that comes within range of our consciousness is subject to our conscious awareness of truth and, therefore, is God-directed, God-maintained, and God-sustained.

The foregoing must not be interpreted as meaning that we can use God to protect us from an accident. We cannot use God to protect us from an accident or from anything else, but we can come into the awareness of God as our being, and, in that being, we shall find no accidents of any kind.

My mind goes back to a very successful businessman who was an earnest seeker of the spiritual way of life. One year he decided to take his family on a holiday over a long Fourth of July week-end. On Friday morning, he was up at five o'clock and spent a full hour in protective prayer, after which he and his family started out on their holiday. The next thing he knew was waking up the following Tuesday morning to find himself and his whole family in a hospital. Not only had the car been demolished, but weeks and months went by before that family was reunited and well.

During the long period of convalescence, uppermost in his mind, was the question, "Why?" But none of his speculations brought a satisfactory answer, so when he had recovered, he sought out someone who had gone a step further on the spiritual path in an endeavor to see if some plausible explanation could be provided. "What happened? Here I am, a very sincere student, and so far as I know there is nothing in my consciousness that should not be there. Why, I even got up an hour ahead of time to do a thorough job of praying for protection. How could this have happened?"

His friend had only one answer, "You invented an accident—you created an accident."

"I don't understand what you are saying. I thought it was important to pray for protection."

"Yes, that is correct, if—. If you had understood the nature of such prayer, all would have been well. But now, let me ask you, what were you protecting yourself from?"

"Well, bad drivers on the road, accidents, and alcohol."

"That's it. You were protecting yourself from a power and a presence apart from God, and you and your family were all going to be rolled up in a nice little ball of cotton where none of that could reach you. But what did you do? You created a mental image of alcohol, accidents, and bad drivers. How do you think it could miss you?"

In that one lesson, this man learned the principle that later made him an outstanding spiritual healer—the lesson that there is only one Power, and that Power is God. To realize God as the mind, life, Soul, Spirit, and substance of the universe, God as the only activity in the consciousness of husband, wife, child, parent, and of anyone who touches our consciousness is protective prayer. It is our protection against the belief that they have a life of their own, and that that life can be in danger. It is our protection against the belief that they have a body of their own that can be impaired or that they have a selfhood apart from God.

Protective prayer consists in knowing that no one has a selfhood apart from God; no one has any mind, life, Soul, Spirit, any being, or any body other than God's. Protection lies in understanding that God is the life, intelligence, Soul, Spirit, immortality, and eternality of every individual on earth. If we do not realize God as *universal* Intelligence, we may feel secure after declaring, as so many metaphysicians do, that God is our intelligence; and then while out driving an automobile have somebody, whose intelligence—so far as our realization is concerned—is not God's, smash into us. Such an accident could not happen if we were realizing God as *universal Intelligence*. What the other automobile driver knows about truth is not of importance; what counts in our experience is how much of truth we know. What we know of truth determines our demonstration, not what the other person knows. It is not enough to say, "I am hid with Christ in God," or "God is my intelligence," or "God is my life." Not at all, because by inference, we are leaving all the rest of the world out, and we are likely to come in contact with that rest of the world sometime or other.

Protective prayer lies in the realization that any truth we know is a universal truth. To fill a child with thoughts of fear by continuous admonitions of a negative nature such as, "Do not do this; do not do that," is a denial of the Christ. Humanly it may be very sensible, and at a certain level of consciousness may be necessary; spiritually it is just the opposite. To give a child a right sense of security, he should be taught that God is indestructible life and intelligence, and that he will always be led in the right way and into the right places. God is the life and the Soul of everybody he meets; and, therefore, no matter whom he meets, he is meeting God. He is always under God's protection and guided by God's wisdom.

Thorough protective prayer consists in realizing God as the mind, the Soul and Spirit, as the substance of the body of every individual; God as the only law unto every individual; God as the life, the immortality and eternality. You have no immortality of your own, and I have no immortality of my own: Whatever immortality we have is the immortality of God made manifest as our eternality and immortality.

There is need for protective prayer. We must protect ourselves at all times from the *acceptance* of the *universal belief* in two powers and in a sense of separation from God. God must become a living experience to us, and we must find a way to make the contact with That from which we have had this sense of separation. When the Spirit touches us, the revelation we receive is that God is. Then we let the Spirit of God take over. We let the divine Presence go before us to make the crooked places straight.

PART FOUR

SPIRITUAL
HEALING:

WITHOUT WORDS
OR THOUGHTS

CHAPTER XV

BEYOND WORDS AND THOUGHTS

Through study, meditation, living with the letter of truth, and constant practice, the principles of spiritual healing become established in consciousness. What is written in this book is intended to speed the transition from a material sense of life to the attainment of that mind which was in Christ Jesus, which is the healing consciousness. Those who are truly spiritually minded and have an understanding of the principles of spiritual healing are able to heal; but being spiritually minded does not mean resting in an intellectual knowledge of these principles; it does not mean making affirmations and denials, or using mental powers or human wisdom.

No person of himself has enough understanding to heal a headache. The Spirit of God that is generated in us, which we have either brought with us to this earth-experience as a divine gift or have attained through the cultivation of it, is that which does the healing. A book such as this is merely an agency to help develop a conscious awareness of that Spirit of God. Success, not only in healing, but in all spiritual demonstration, is something that far trancends any knowledge that we have or may acquire. True, the knowledge that we acquire does serve a purpose, but that purpose is only to lead us into the actual spiritual consciousness.

It is difficult for many metaphysicians to believe that

167

all the truth they know and all the truth they study is not God-power and does not bring God into their experience, nor does it give them God-guidance, God-health, or God-strength. The average student really believes that reading books, going to church, or going to classes somehow sets him apart in God's eyes. It is better, of course, to do these things than not to do them, but spiritual truth becomes a law of God in our experience only in proportion to our *realization* of it. Never forget that. There must first be the acknowledgment, and then must come the realization.

We may study truth for a year and have a realization on some specific point, and then on that particular point, we can rest in God-government, not that God divides Himself, but that we have seen only in part—"For now we see through a glass darkly; but then face to face." But the "glass darkly" does not immediately disappear, although with each point of realization the glass becomes lighter and lighter until in the end it is a perfect transparency, and we see God face to face.

For example, many of us on this path have had the experience of beginning the study of some spiritual teaching and catching a glimpse of God as Life. At first, we may only repeat that as words, intellectually agreeing to its truth. Eventually, however, a point of transition comes and we realize:

God is life. My limited human sense of life is now gone: There is no longer a need to demonstrate health; there is no longer age, and, therefore, there is no youth to demonstrate. My life is not mine: My life is God's, and that life is always lived at the standpoint of infinity and eternality.

The moment we can see that God is life or that Life is God, from then on our physical condition begins to improve. That may not improve our supply, however; but one day we may have a similar experience with supply and catch the vision of supply as not something we can get, but as something already established within us. When that realization comes, there is no further need for a demonstration of supply.

All the truth that we read in the Bible and in books of spiritual wisdom is only true in proportion to our realization of it: We may have beautiful demonstrations through the spiritually illumined, but we are only borrowing their oil and benefiting by their state of consciousness. That is legitimate for the new or young student, and it is effective up to a certain point; but if we do not awaken and ourselves become spiritually illumined, we shall be among those who will be saying twenty years from now that at one time we had wonderful demonstrations, but it does not happen to us any more.

Let us remember that spiritual truth can be likened to a checking account. We cannot draw out more than we have deposited. Truth is infinite, but demonstrated truth is only in proportion to the effort, the devotion, the love, the labor, and the sacrifice that we put into attaining the realization of it. It takes effort; it takes work. It is a labor of love; and, therefore, the person who does not love it and the person who does not labor with his love will not draw out any more than the little time, work, effort, or money he has put into it. Studying, reading, meditating, pondering, hearing—these are all steps which ultimately lead us to say, "Whereas I was blind, now I see."

Actual spiritual healing work is based on the fact that no amount of truth that we can know about God or man is going to solve a problem or heal a disease: All it will do is to quiet us until we can get into such a peaceful atmosphere that we really feel ourselves floating in God, not asleep and not dead—nothing like that—not a form of hypnosis where we are halfway between two worlds: It is a peace that is an aliveness, a tingling; it is the peace that passes understanding. In this state we cannot go to sleep; we shall never want to sleep again, but shall want to stay awake forever and forever and forever in that state of aliveness. It is an alertness, and yet is peaceful and quiet.

It is when we are in this absolute quiet that something happens, something which bursts the bubble, and when we emerge from it, within minutes or hours or days, we find that our problem has dissolved.

It has dissolved because the problem, whatever its name or nature, was a mentally created image based on a material sense of law and life. We may have called it the law of karma or the Christian law of cause and effect—"Whatsoever a man soweth, that shall he also reap. For he that soweth to his flesh shall of the flesh reap corruption; but he that soweth to the Spirit shall of the Spirit reap life everlasting"—but let us remember that "the law was given by Moses"—the law of karma, the law of cause and effect —"but grace and truth came by Jesus Christ."

The law is for those who live humanly; grace is for those who live spiritually. The very moment that we are willing to let go of the law of self-preservation, the law of self-righteousness, the law of self-condemnation, the law of condemnation of others, and abide in love, that is, abide in the feeling that God is equally the parent of all and that as children of God we love and share with each other, then we shall find that a transition takes place in our lives. Then we shall no more be guilty of trying to demonstrate supply than we would be of stealing it, because we would understand that to attempt to demonstrate it would be merely trying to take it out of this world of effect where probably it now belongs to somebody else but where tomorrow we hope it will belong to us.

Never again will we seek anything that is already in the world of effect. We shall be satisfied to have our good come to us out of the Infinite Invisible. We shall be satisfied to be patient and wait until we can demonstrate the presence of God knowing that the realization of that Presence is fulfillment. The key word is "fulfillment." This fulfillment manifests not out of what already *exists*, but out of what the

Father sends forth from within us, even though it will appear in some human or material form in the without.

Spiritually we are infinite, spiritually we are as infinite as God; and so it is a sin to desire anything. Let us ask only that God give Himself to us, blessing us with His grace: This is asking, knocking, and receiving; this is the only legitimate desire. But when we reduce our desire—our asking, knocking, seeking—to some form of material good, we are under a material sense of law. It has been claimed that Moses himself did not reach the Promised Land because he sought a demonstration of water. Moses was determined to get water out of a rock, and because he tapped that rock for water and made an exhibition of his power, he was refused admittance to the Promised Land.

When the Master was hungered and was tempted to demonstrate food, his response was, "Oh, no! Get thee behind me, Satan! I will make no personal demonstration." Three times he was tempted to use his personal powers; three times he refused. "No, it is God's function to supply me; it is God's function to have dominion, not mine," and in resisting the temptation to demonstrate things, he proved that he was above the law of mind and matter. He had entered the realm of pure Spirit, the kingdom of God, in which "it is your Father's good pleasure to give you the kingdom"—not to give us a *method* of getting the Kingdom, but to give us the *Kingdom.*

Whatever degree of suffering there is in this world is due to being under a material sense of law. When we meet with any physical or mental law, we should return to the principle and wipe it out with the understanding that it is not power because God is the only power.

God is a jealous God, and God does not give His power to you or me. Just as the inspiration which comes to any creative worker is not his inspiration, but God's, merely flowing *through* him, so God's power flows *through* you or me. When a man thinks that any gift that he has is his own, in a few short years, it is exhausted, depleted—he is all dried up, and he wonders why new ideas are not flowing. That is because he claimed them as his own; he believed they were his unique possession; he believed that God had bestowed a special favor upon him by giving him this talent.

God never gives His talent to anybody. God maintains His talent within Himself and expresses it freely and joyously through us, but it always remains God's talent. Those who know this never run dry; they never run out of inspiration because the inspiration is never theirs; it is God's, and they are but the instrument through which it appears on earth. When there is a restricted inspiration, when there is a restricted supply of anything—health, money, or opportunity—always remember this: Some universal sense of law is in operation, and we are under that law and are suffering because we believe that we are creators instead of realizing that there is only one Creator.

This sense of a dual creation has its basis in the ego. In the Garden of Eden, Adam began to believe that he and Eve were creators. Today man has discovered his mind and thinks that he can create his good mentally, or that he can create evil with that same mind. In the end it must be recognized that man is not a creator. He may be the instrument through which the creative Principle functions, but he, himself, is not a creator.

No man or woman was given the gift of creating his or her good mentally or destroying good mentally: The ego is in the chair when anyone believes that he is a mental creator just as it is when he believes that he is a physical creator. When all claims to being a creator are relinquished, and when it is realized that all things that are manifested and do appear are made from things which are not seen, then are we living in the invisible realm. All things that are made —all things, including our body—will be harmonious. It is only while the belief lasts—the universal belief that we are creators with a selfhood apart from God—that the body, our relationships, and our affairs remain inharmonious and discordant.

Watch the miracle when we give up believing in God *over* error or Love *over* hate and accept wholeheartedly the principle of one power. Watch the miracle that comes into our lives when we stop defending ourselves against shadows on the wall—nothingness—when we stop fighting the errors of the world, the tyrants and the powers of the world.

Watch what happens when you and I can reach the state of consciousness which recognizes the enemy as but the "arm of flesh." No matter how big or how strong it seems to be, it is only the "arm of flesh"—nothingness. "The battle is not yours, but God's. . . . Stand ye still"; there is but one Power. Agree with your adversary: Do not affirm; do not deny. Sit still, become peaceful, and wait for the word of God to come, and when it comes, it will be strong and powerful and sharper than a two-edged sword.

Our knowledge will never be sharper than a two-edged sword. *Our* thoughts and *our* powers of concentration will never perform miracles, but by living these principles we become witnesses to the miracle of grace. Therefore, let us take certain principles and begin to live them now. Let us begin with the very important principle of one power:

God is the only power. Therefore, I shall not fear what mortal man can do to me. I shall not fear germs, infection, or contagion, nor shall I fear the governments of man. Only one thing is power, the Infinite Invisible.

If we can hold to that, our way will be made harmonious. It does not mean that we shall succeed 100 per cent of the time because the pressure of the world is so great —newspapers, radios, television, gossip, rumor—that it hypnotizes us into the temptation to accept a power apart from God. However, the fact that we may fall down once in awhile is nothing of which to be ashamed or to fear. Everybody in the world has had moments when the temptations of the world have crept in and convinced him that there were powers outside his own being.

Tell me who has ever been completely free from all temptation. Jesus was tempted. Temptations have come to all the great masters and to their disciples. Temptations come to everyone to accept a world apart from God's world, a power apart from God's power, pleasures apart from God's pleasures, prophets apart from God's prophets. If it should happen to us in one form or another, let us recognize it as temptation, pick ourselves up, start over again, standing on the truth of *God as the one and only power,* and continue in a state of receptivity, letting God reveal Itself in us and through us, satisfied that if we are evidencing some measure of God in our experience, we are doing well.

Every time we engage in any healing activity, we are acknowledging that of our own selves we can do nothing, but that the allness and the fullness and completeness of the Father can pour through us and raise the dead, heal the sick, and feed the hungry:

I of mine own self am nothing, but because I and the Father are one, the allness and the fullness of the Father is made manifest through me and as me. Therefore, wherever I go, the glory of God goes before me to shine, to make Its presence felt.

As we maintain that emptiness of self, always beginning our day with that realization, we shall soon see that even the flowers will bloom in our presence, because our presence will be a continuous state of benediction even to those who do not know who we are, or what we are, or why.

CHAPTER XVI

IS

The basis of all spiritual teaching is that spiritual consciousness evolves in what is called "time." We may wonder why time enters into that which is eternity and which knows no such thing as time, but the element of time is involved because spiritual evolution is the unfolding of consciousness, which to our sense appears as time. However, there is a definite moment in time and space when each one of us makes the transition from law to grace. Up to that point, we are students of truth, seekers after God; and through our study and good works, we hope and expect to improve our human situation.

The Hindus liken this process of spiritual evolution to the peeling away of the skins of an onion. The peeling away of one layer of skin is barely perceptible, but by the time ten or fifteen layers have been removed, a definite change is noticeable. As the skins are removed, layer by layer, eventually a place is reached where there are no more onion skins: There is only nothingness; the onion is no more. And so it is that human beings are born into this world, bringing with them numbers of layers of material sense to which they continually add, building up the onion-self, skin by skin, until they begin the return journey to the Father's house.

When that spiritual impulse is felt, then we begin to study and meditate, always with the goal that one day we may actually feel God within us, realize the Presence, be touched by Him, and come to live under grace in that state of consciousness in which there is no longer any law—no longer a law of good and evil, no longer a law of cause and effect, no longer a law of punishment and reward: There is only a state of grace—and at a certain moment in our experience, it happens.

Such an experience takes place in time. It may happen at ten o'clock in the morning, at midnight, or in the silence of the early morning hours, but at some time or other it does take place, and we feel that inner impulsion and know that we have felt it. Then we relax, or more accurately It relaxes us. It relaxes us to such an extent that we never again feel a responsibility for our own life.

In fact, if it really happens, we no longer care whether we live our life on this side of the grave or on the other—actually it could make no difference because life is eternal, immortal. Neither do we concern ourselves with whether we have a certain amount of dollars left over at the end of the day with which to begin tomorrow, because every moment of every day is lived under grace. It is perfectly all right to have a million dollars, if life unfolds in that direction, but it would not concern us if there were nothing left over. Every moment is provided for by the grace of that moment.

We can know how far we are from attaining spiritual consciousness by how much we live in the future; we can know how far we are from attaining even good normal humanhood by how much we live in the past. Only a very, very mortal, material state of consciousness lives much in the past, either in the glories of the past, or its sins or diseases. Only a low state of thought concerns itself overly much with the past except as the past may have lessons for the present, or for the future. But otherwise, dwelling in the past, immersing or dousing oneself in either its glories or miseries, merely indicates a great, great distance in consciousness from that spiritual estate which lives by grace.

The degree of humanhood also can be measured by the

extent to which one lives in the future. Spiritual being has no future: Spiritual being means living this moment, relaxing in it, rejoicing in it, sharing whatever there is of this moment.

Can you imagine trying to live a minute from now? A minute from now is a complete vacuum: It has nothing in it and nobody in it. What pleasure can there be in an hour from now? And on the other hand, how can we be concerned for an hour from now when we do not know what God's plan is for us an hour from now? How do we know how the rent is to be met on the first of the month or how do we know that the fuel will not be in the basement at the proper time? How do we know God's plan?

When we are fearful, we are declaring that God has no plan for us and we are virtually saying, "I am counting on making my demonstration without the help of God." As a matter of fact, if we understood that life is God's demonstration and not ours, we would not be concerned whether we were cold or warm, hungry or fed. Is not God capable of maintaining Himself as His own image and likeness?

We cannot live an hour ago. Try it and see if you do not pull yourself to pieces. Try to live an hour from now and see whether you can move yourself forward in time: You cannot—you only make yourself miserable by wondering what might happen when that hour arrives. Begin to live in the now. This living in the now does not shut our eyes to the fact that tomorrow will also be now, but rather makes us realize that that which is a seed at this moment will in its nowness be a bud; and when it is a bud, it will in its nowness become a full-blown flower. That is living in the now. But to concern ourselves with whether or not the seed will ever become a rose is living in the future.

This is God's universe, the universe of Spirit, and if we do not live in the universe of Spirit, but insist rather on tabernacling in "this world," then we withdraw ourselves from "My kingdom," from the kingdom of God. When we

are living in time—the past or the future—we remove ourselves from the kingdom of heaven. There is no kingdom
of heaven yesterday, and there is no kingdom of heaven tomorrow. The kingdom of heaven is a state of grace which
can only be experienced now. That now may be three o'clock
or eight o'clock or twelve o'clock, but it is always *now*. To
go back to an hour ago in memory or to concern ourselves
with tomorrow is deliberately to remove ourselves from the
kingdom of heaven. But to live in the realization that, this
second, God is expressing Itself, God is fulfilling Its own
destiny, is to live in the kingdom of heaven here on earth.

When I say that there is a point of transition in time
when we pass from speaking these words, reading or hearing
them, to living them, I mean that at some specific moment
in time, a change of consciousness takes place within us
when this becomes a living truth, not one heard with the
ears, not one read with the eyes, but a living, demonstrable
truth in which we become stabilized and from which we
never move.

This transition into a consciousness of nowness is a
state of grace in which we relax and realize that henceforth
we do not live by physical might or mental powers, but that
we live by divine grace and that not of ourselves, but of
God. It is not human wisdom or any truth that we know
that will bring it about; our wisdom and our truth will
merely be the reminders to hold us to that "straight and
narrow" way.

The way is straight and narrow because it can only exist
in the now. The minute we deviate into the past or future,
we have lost the way. It is so straight and narrow that it
can only be lived now—*now, the eternal now!*

Whether the body is in pain or whether the pocketbook
is empty or even whether the state of morals is not too
admirable has nothing to do with it. Those conditions are
merely the effects of world hypnotism still operating in
consciousness, and they will be dispelled when this moment

of transition takes place, when we come into the infinite Way, the Way of life, the Way which I *am*.

Whatever our spiritual or religious background, it should never be necessary for us to ask the question, "What is the Way?" Lao-tze speaks of the Way; Buddha speaks of the Path; Jesus Christ speaks of the Way. What is this Way? All three answer, "I *am*." Probably in our day it would be easier to understand this if we used the big little word, IS. In other words, now I am—not I was, not I will be, not I shall be, not I ought to be, or I deserve to be. The Way is, IS: I *am*.

I *am* means that I already am in heaven; I already am perfect; I already am spiritual. All this is implied in the words, "I am." In our seeking and searching days, however, it is necessary to declare the principle even if we are not demonstrating it; just as when the study of music is begun, the student must abide by its principles even if he cannot strike the right notes in time or space. Similarly, no matter how incorrectly a student works out his mathematical problems, he still must hold to the principle of mathematics. He may score only 50 per cent on an examination, and later may raise that score to 90, but 90 or even 99 is not good in mathematics. It has to be 100 per cent; otherwise it is incorrect.

And so it is that in the beginning of our spiritual healing work, we would be very much discouraged if we were expected to achieve 100 per cent success. Despite the fact that we are not outwardly manifesting that degree of success in demonstration, we do know the goal: The goal is not the attainment of an improved humanhood; the goal is the attainment of that mind which was in Christ Jesus; the goal is the attainment of "My kingdom" which is not of this world.

That is the goal, and the principle is I *am*. We now know the Way: The Way is I AM. I am the Way. I am now the Way. IS! The grace of God *is*. That is the straight

and narrow truth which we must hug to us until in a moment
that we know not of, in a moment that we think not, the
bridegroom comes, and the spiritual realization dawns. But,
until that moment, we have to cling to the Way, and the
Way is *I Am:* The Way is, IS; the Way is this eternal moment; the Way is dropping concern about yesterday or tomorrow; the Way is to face fearlessly this moment—face ourselves
in this moment and realize that it is in this moment that
all that God is, I am.

Because the Way is so straight and narrow, all this is
difficult. We have to give up yesterday, and we have to give
up tomorrow. True, it is difficult, but no purpose is served
in saying, "It is difficult"; no purpose is served in complain-
ing, "But it is so hard." What difference does it make how
hard it is? Everybody has had difficulties, but there is no use
talking about them because few care very much about anyone else's hardships. On the other hand, if we are finding
the way easy, telling our neighbors about it or boasting of
our success, this just adds to their burdens if they are meeting
with adversity.

Each one has to follow the Way as it is given to him. Each
one has to walk this Way alone. It is not an easy way.
Nobody has ever said that it was easy, and least of all, would
I ever claim that it is easy. I know what it means to pass
from the mental or intellectual perception of a truth to
the spiritual discernment of it. I know what it means to
think, "Yes, you keep telling me these marvelous truths,
but nothing is happening in my life." I know what that
means; I have gone through it. I remember hearing these
very same truths and thinking, "I don't see any truth in
it at all. What is it doing for me or for my neighbors?"

This is not an easy way, but when a person comes to this
work with a completely open mind, he can receive its light.
However, if he comes with some area of consciousness blocked
off, judging this to be good and that to be bad, he is thinking in terms of the past or the future, and it is almost an

impossibility for the complete light to reach him. If we are thinking in terms of the past or the future, we are thinking in terms of both good and evil, right and wrong, saint and sinner. The person seeking the full light must realize and recognize that, in this split second of time, there is only *now*—the now in which *I Am*.

As this spiritual sense is realized, we do not *overcome* jealousy, envy, sensuality; rather do we come into a kingdom where none of these things exists because there is no personal sense to be catered to, to receive anything, to need anything, or to want anything. How can anything be given to a person who has attained? How can a person who has attained have anything left to desire? How can a person who has attained have any sense of incompleteness?

In that attainment which takes place in a split second of transition, God is revealed as fulfillment. There is a Center within us which unfolds spiritually, and, as It unfolds, It provides for our daily needs. However material the object may be that is necessary to our immediate unfoldment —healing, dollars, bread and butter, meat, housing, transportation—whatever its nature, it is not necessary to take thought about its attainment or unfoldment. It will appear automatically as it is needed.

This Spirit within us will always appear in visible expression the moment it is needed, and It will appear *as the form* necessary at that moment, whether it is the form of honesty that gives back the missing two dollars, the form of a loaf of bread, or the form of a seat in an airplane. Whatever form is necessary, and irrespective of how physical or material it may seem to our sense, it will be there—it will be there in proportion as we relinquish the word "I." I— the personal sense of I—am not responsible for my daily bread: *I am*; God is; the Spirit is. If we cling to the personal sense of "I," then we do not permit the Spirit to operate and flow through us as healing and regeneration.

All already exists at the standpoint of fulfillment, and

so there are no desires, there is no future: There is only this second, lived twenty-four hours a day, in which nothing can be added to us and nothing can be taken from us. That is a high point of spiritual unfoldment. Then there is no desire because there is fulfillment, and in fulfillment what is left to be desired? What can we hope to get? What can be withheld from us? Nothing!

CHAPTER XVII

IF I BE LIFTED UP

Now we have done with words and thoughts and have entered that place of communion with God. "Yet in my flesh shall I see God." When? When we are still; when we have obeyed the First Commandment, recognizing only one power and acknowledging God as the central theme of our being; when we have loosed all erroneous concepts, as but the "arm of flesh," nothingness; then we stand in that consciousness of oneness and let the light within us shine.

The weapons of human belief—human concepts and human thoughts—have no power against that person who has consciously realized his oneness with God and his oneness with everything on every level of life. There need be no words and no thoughts; there must only be the inner *feel* of that union which may express itself as words.

All that God is, I am. Thou seest me; thou seest the Father shining right through me, for I and the Father are one: I in Him, and He in me; I in you, and you in me; and all one in Christ Jesus—in spiritual being, in spiritual sonship and identity. There is nothing in this world antagonistic to me, and I am antagonistic to nothing in this world because my oneness with the Father constitutes my oneness with all spiritual being.

God speaks the universal language of Spirit: We may hear God actually as a voice in our ear, or we may see God as light, or as a form; but on the other hand we may feel God only as a release, a warmth, or as a lifting in consciousness. There will be a sign; there will be a signal—*but no sign shall be given in advance*: These signs shall *follow* them that have this conscious awareness! Therefore, our prayer in its highest sense is the prayer of contact, the prayer of communion, in which no words or thoughts pass from us to God, and there may not even be words or thoughts from God to us, but there will be an awareness, there will be a sense of communion, an inner peace.

True prayer comes to its completeness and perfection when there is no desire; it comes to full bloom in this feeling of communion when all sense of desire for anything has been laid aside. It is just as if it were Christmas morning at the tree and we had received all our gifts—all our wishes have been granted, and now all that remains is a feeling of, "Thank you, everyone."

When our consciousness is lifted to that sense of "Thank You, Father; thank you, everyone," then comes the fullness and completeness of communion with God, and in that there is a resting in the Soul. As a baby rests in its mother's arms, so does that resting in the Soul come to us. But the infant has no desires; it has no wants, no needs: It is at rest. So do we come to a period of refreshment and a rest in the realization that it is the Father's good pleasure to give us the kingdom. With that we rest, never seeking—not even inwardly desiring—but rather relaxing in the Spirit.

That leads to a state of consciousness which in The Infinite Way is called "the beholder." It is as if we were sitting at peace watching the activity of the day take place: We may be up early in the morning and watch the sun rise; we may go out into the garden and watch the flowers come into bloom; we may sit down at our desks and watch our mail being answered; and as a call comes for help, we sit in this communion and watch God pray in us—watch that communion dissolve the appearance and restore harmony.

At every period of the day we are the beholder. We do not strive for supply: We behold supply as it unfolds infinitely from the one Source. We never pray for health: We become still; we rest in this prayer of the Soul while we nestle in Its warmth and watch as the health appears or the opportunities unfold. Always we must remember that we are not seeking to have our nets filled. Empty nets no longer fill us with anxious concern. We have passed beyond that into the realm where our only desire is to behold God's spiritual universe and to tabernacle with the sons and daughters of God:

The Father knoweth my needs, and I stand here as a beholder, not praying for opportunity tomorrow, but sitting quietly in this atmosphere of the Soul watching my opportunity come to me. Just as the rivers flow to the sea, their activity governed by some law of God because it is the normal natural thing for a river to do—to flow to the sea to feed the vast oceans of our earth—so it is the normal and natural thing that God's grace flow to me. It has been dammed up by desire, fear, doubt, and by believing that God was something separate and apart from my being and was not aware of my needs. Now, I release all concern and stand as a beholder of God's infinite goodness.

Our prayer is a peace-be-still, a silent communion—even unto that storm at sea. The Master never prayed that it be dispelled: His only prayer was, "Be still." Was he addressing the water? No, he was addressing his consciousness and the consciousness of his disciples, "Peace, be still." If our consciousness is still, there are no stormy waters within or without. If our consciousness is still, everything about us takes on the complexion of that stillness.

Our need is for one thing alone—conscious communion with God. That is the highest form of prayer, and that form of prayer can only take place after we have learned, first of all, that God is, and, secondly, that all that exists in this universe is God "is-ing"—Is, Is, Is. That *Is*, is neither human good nor human ill; It is neither human health nor human sickness: It is just a spiritual Is.

When we have worked with these principles until we come to a point where we no longer put up even a mental defense against the problems besetting us, but like David walk out without armor in the name of God—when that time comes, our prayers and treatment will be performed without words and without thought. There is no need for a word or a thought in giving a treatment after we have learned to "loose him, and let him go," never holding person, thing, or condition in judgment or condemnation.

In quietness and in stillness shall be our strength—not in speech. Speech is our human way of interpreting divine ideas, but the divine ideas express and manifest themselves within us without words. We put the finger on the lips, are still, and receive an assurance that God is on the field, that the battle is not ours but God's—*that there is no battle*.

It becomes the responsibility and privilege of every person to lift the world in some measure above its present level of consciousness. Those who do not yet know these principles or have not demonstrated them to some degree have a right to look to us for help. And we have the right and responsibility to say, "Yes, I can give you help"—not because we are more spiritual or have certain powers that someone else does not have, but because we know the truth. Knowing the truth is what makes those who turn to us free.

It becomes our further responsibility, if we are serious students, to begin to let our own problems alone, to stop praying about them and begin to pray for others—to let our own erroneous beliefs, or stumbling blocks, be dissolved through the truth that we are knowing for the world or for those who call upon us. To the human being living from a material sense of life, it is very important that he be healthy and that he have a goodly measure of supply—an ample measure—and that he have friends and relatives. Not so with the truth-student! He has no right to be swayed, influenced, or controlled by the ordinary standards of the world; he should have no concern as to the state of his body, purse, or affairs. What difference does any of that make? There is only one really important thing: "Do I know God? Have I reached a point in my life where I can know God? What difference does it make how healthy I am, if I have not yet known God, if I have not seen Him face to face?"

As we continue in our study, we are bound to have healings —healings of ourselves and of others. Even the healing of a simple headache should be enough to prove that the presence of God is active in our experience, here and now. There ought never to be a need for another healing after that because we should then recognize, "Now, I know that there is a possibility of bringing God into my experience; now it has been proved to me; and now I dedicate my life to this purpose." With months or years of such devotion, the day will come when seldom, if ever, would we have to turn to anyone else for help.

There are times during moments of stress, however, when everyone may have to do that. The Master did it when he asked the eleven disciples to stay awake with him, and he must have expected help of his disciples when he was on the Cross. It is undoubtedly right that, when in distress, we should feel free to turn to one another occasionally. That is why we are on the same path together. That is why spiritually we are brothers and sisters to each other: Spiritually we are one and of one household.

Once we meet God face to face and know what the presence of God does in our lives, from then on we live only for one purpose—*to live in that Presence.* From then on we do not have any problems to work out; we have God to know aright. Every truth-student would do well to give up all attempts to solve his own individual problems in the pursuit of the one great purpose: "What difference does it make whether my problems are solved or unsolved, if I have not yet come to know God aright? I have only one problem now: to know Him aright, whom to know aright is life eternal. Once I know God, I have no problems."

A person who knows one statement of truth can give a treatment to any claim that exists; and, if he has sufficient courage and conviction, it would not make any difference if it were cancer, consumption, or polio. One statement of truth! That is all that is required for healing. If just one truth were pondered, eventually the inner meaning of that statement, that which we call the realization or the discernment of that statement, would come to life and would heal anything. As a rule, what happens in that pondering is that one statement gives birth to another, following in sequence, and leading up to some final conclusion which clears the whole situation.

You and I cannot perform miracles—no human being can do that. However, if we can be humble enough to minimize the importance of our own understanding and magnify and exalt God's understanding, such a truth will come through as would raise the dead. Even if we do not know any statement of truth, we can still heal if we are willing to be quiet and receptive enough until He utters His voice through us. It will not be our word, but the word of God, and that Word is quick and sharp and powerful.

There is not a person reading this book who should not be ready to accept the responsibility of beginning to heal now. It is not your spirituality or mine that will heal anybody; it is not your understanding or mine that is going to heal: It is God's understanding to which we make ourselves receptive by becoming still. As these truths begin to work in consciousness, we shall find that they are working in the consciousness of our patients and students and of the world at large.

Our function is to lift the consciousness of those who come to us high enough above the storms of human sense to where they, too, may feel the divine harmony flooding their being and body. "I, if I be lifted up from the earth, will draw all men unto me." This is not a task; this is not labor, because we do not have to reach out to people in order to lift them up. We have only to retire into our own sanctuary and find this peace, and when it has been found, our household and all those who are attuned to us take on a measure of that same peace in proportion to their receptivity. Some may hold themselves outside of this peace because at their present state of unfoldment they are not receptive to the voice of God, but nevertheless the time will come when every man will be taught of God.

It is not for us to be concerned with who responds to the spiritual impulse, but to be so lifted in consciousness that all those who come to us may partake of the bread—the spiritual bread—the wine and the water, not that it is to be forced upon anyone, but that everyone with an open consciousness may receive it. To those in our household, whether receptive and responsive to truth or not, we owe the obligation never to come into their presence except in the highest degree of consciousness possible to us at the moment; we owe this to ourselves, and we owe it to the Father who has lifted us above the storms of the human world. When we were ignorant of this truth it was not demanded of us, but to him that hath much shall be expected, much shall be demanded.

So in the measure of our enlightenment we now take upon our shoulders a responsibility from which we can never be released. The God whose grace gave us this light expects that we shall shed that light—not by proselyting, not by seeking people, but by maintaining ourselves at a high spiritual level, even if no one in our world knows what we are doing.

We already know the secret: The Father is in me, and I am in Him, and we are in each other. That secret we know. Now without any words and without any thoughts, twice a day, three times a day, four times a day, and by next year twenty times a day, we must go within, if only for half a minute, to acknowledge the Presence, to feel the divine Energy, the divine Spark, and so live that all men coming within range of our consciousness feel the outpouring of God upon them.

We are God's instruments; we are God's servants. The Son of God is always the servant of his fellow-man, forever at the service of those who call. Earthly kings are served, but spiritual kings are servants. No one should ever boast or brag of divine sonship because divine sonship bestows a humility which recognizes that only the light of God can lift the consciousness of those who come to us to that place where they can behold the Father face to face. As servants of the most High, we remain in the world, unaffected by its passions, hates, or loves, unaffected by its wars or intervals between wars: We remain in it as a blessing.